Praise for *High Ten*

"On every team across every sport and every business, a cohesive and inclusive culture remains the most fundamental objective. When a coach or leader wins the team's heart and respect, success always follows closely behind. For building a powerful culture, I give this book a High Ten!"
— *Howie Long, NFL Hall of Fame, Super Bowl Champion and eight-time Pro Bowl, Analyst Fox Sports*

"Respect, inclusion, and teamwork are at the foundation of every great team. These winning hallmarks can also be difficult for a coach or leader to develop. Martin's book gives you the tools to identify and solve some of the biggest challenges facing your team."
— *Kyle Shanahan, Head Coach, San Francisco 49ers*

"MMA is the epitome of an individual sport, but I learned it takes a team to get you properly prepared. A positive culture can make an average team reach for excellence and a negative culture can bring down the best. This book will help you build a team to succeed."
— *Forrest Griffin, UFC Light Heavyweight Champion and Hall of Fame, Vice President of Athlete Development, UFC Performance Center*

"Successful enterprises are built on an organizational culture that empowers everyone to embrace the purpose of a day as if they are part of a movement or a cause. High Ten lays out how to forge the warrior spirit that defines highly successful teams."
— *Don Katz, Audible Founder and Executive Chairman*

"Winning at the highest level is not one or two big things, it's a thousand little things done right. The details of culture are first and foremost. Culture is the heart and soul of every great team and cannot be left to chance. High Ten proves culture is not an accident; it's an action."

– Phil Simms, Superbowl MVP, CBS Sports Analyst

"As the leader of any organization or team, developing a culture of trust and discipline is your number one priority. There are few things as satisfying as working toward a common goal with a team of people you appreciate and admire. Read this book and you will be on your way to building that type of team."

– Lieutenant General Anthony Burshnick, US Air Force (Retired), 12th Commandant of the United States Air Force Academy

"Culture is a powerful force that improves teamwork and creates sustained success. If you want to improve your team, business, or relationships, read this book!"

– Jon Gordon, bestselling author of The Energy Bus *and* The Power of Positive Leadership

"Being part of a great team gives you confidence and direction as an athlete. To be side by side with a teammate chasing greatness creates a culture of winning. Let *High Ten* show you how to be a better leader of culture."

– Frankie Edgar, UFC Lightweight Champion

"*High Ten* proves that to achieve success in an industry that is both uniquely collaborative and highly competitive, it's critical to build a team that feels respected, trusted, appreciated, and heard. That feels cared for and inspired. If you can create that environment, anything is possible – absolutely anything!"

– Karen Baker Landers, two-time Oscar winner for Best Sound, The Bourne Ultimatum *and* Skyfall

"High Ten is a culture bedrock from which to build any organization or team. Through gripping stories and an experienced lens, this will have every leader ready to positively impact their own environments and better cultivate future success."

– Casey Brown, Head Coach,
University of Pennsylvania Women's Soccer,
Patriot League Coach of the Year, All-American and
WPS Soccer Draftee

"Few people recognize racing as a team sport, but a group of athletes, engineers, mechanics, and a driver all contribute individual talents to drive the team's success. Successful teams have an unselfish culture where teammates can challenge each other to grow while holding each other accountable to the mission. *High Ten* can help you build that type of team."

– Jeremy Bullins, NASCAR Crew Chief, Team Penske

"Everyone knows culture is at the core of every great team, but few people know how to build it. *High Ten* is your blueprint for assessing and adjusting your current culture. If you are a leader in any capacity, let Martin help turn your team into a great group of fire-breathing dragons!"

– Todd Durkin, MA, CSCS, Founder, Fitness Quest 10, CEO,
Todd Durkin Enterprises, IDEA and ACE,
Trainer of the Year, author of The Impact Body Plan *and*
Get Your Mind Right

"Culture is the backbone of any team or organization. A weak one will crumble, while a strong one will give a unified purpose to all and help you achieve your ultimate goals. *High Ten* will make your culture-game strong!"

– Claus Souza, Assistant Strength and
Conditioning Coach, Denver Nuggets

"*Both hands on deck!* Martin Rooney is once again *on point* and on fire. In his latest book, *High Ten*, he clarifies business culture, team productivity, and personal inspiration that you can take to a new level of success. This 'story within a story' will leave you and your team members blessed, changed for the better, and in position to win."

       — *Jeffrey Gitomer, bestselling author of* Get Sh*t Done *and*
             The Little Red Book of Selling

"The building of a team and a culture is driven by trust. Embracing and genuinely loving one another is the method by which trust is built. Martin Rooney's book shows you how to build the kind of trust necessary to create a winning team."

          — *Matthew Driscoll, Head Coach,*
   University of North Florida Men's Basketball, winningest coach in
       program history, three-time ASUN Coach of the Year

"I've coached teams from four different nations and culture is the most important step in building a team. If the team is not on the same page culturally, working together toward a common goal is extremely hard. Let Martin's book help you find the Keepers and lose your Vultures."

          — *Todd Hays, Olympic Silver Medalist,*
        Coach to 6 Olympic Medalists and
          13 World Championship Medalists,
          Head Coach Bobsleigh Canada

HIGH
TEN

MARTIN ROONEY

AUTHOR OF *COACH TO COACH*

HIGH TEN

AN INSPIRING STORY ABOUT BUILDING GREAT TEAM CULTURE

WILEY

Published by John Wiley & Sons, Inc., Hoboken, New Jersey.

Published simultaneously in Canada.

For general information on our other products and services or for technical support, please contact our Customer Care Department within the United States at (800) 762-2974, outside the United States at (317) 572-3993 or fax (317) 572-4002.

Wiley publishes in a variety of print and electronic formats and by print-on-demand. Some material included with standard print versions of this book may not be included in e-books or in print-on-demand. If this book refers to media such as a CD or DVD that is not included in the version you purchased, you may download this material at http://booksupport.wiley.com. For more information about Wiley products, visit www.wiley.com.

Library of Congress Cataloging-in-Publication Data

Names: Rooney, Martin, 1971- author. | John Wiley & Sons, publisher.
Title: High ten : an inspiring story about building great team culture / Martin Rooney.
Description: Hoboken, New Jersey : Wiley, [2021] | Includes index.
Identifiers: LCCN 2021011332 (print) | LCCN 2021011333 (ebook) | ISBN 9781119806165 (hardback) | ISBN 9781119806189 (adobe pdf) | ISBN 9781119806172 (epub)
Subjects: LCSH: Corporate culture. | Personnel management. | Mentoring. | Coaching (Athletics).
Classification: LCC HD58.7 .R665 2021 (print) | LCC HD58.7 (ebook) | DDC 658.4/022—dc23
LC record available at https://lccn.loc.gov/2021011332
LC ebook record available at https://lccn.loc.gov/2021011333

Cover Design: Wiley
Cover Image: © PremiumVector/Shutterstock

SKY1007224_052121

To the great Dr. Rob Gilbert, who taught me the best person on the team is the best person for the team.

Contents

Foreword

Bottom line – great leaders focus on establishing great cultures! In *High Ten*, Martin Rooney tells an inspiring story about how to build a great team with a great culture, and he shares lessons and insights that will work anywhere: at home, in the military, on sports teams, or in corporate America. In the Army, our leaders are expected to provide purpose, direction, and motivation to their soldiers, and as commanders they are explicitly responsible for the culture of their units. But the very best commanders find a way for those in the unit to also "own" the culture – so it's everyone's responsibility. Martin drives this point home and then some.

Throughout my Army career, I've learned and observed that when building a culture, the foundation is character and values. These are essential to building trust, which leads to cohesive teams. Teams where people feel like they are part of something, not just in something. Teams that are loyal to one another and also to their values. Teams that are disciplined and whose standards exemplify excellence, and they hold one another accountable in meeting or exceeding those standards. Doing otherwise would be an acceptance of mediocrity, and that doesn't equate to winning on the battlefield, playing field, or in life. Strong cohesion also results in extraordinary resiliency, and teams that are able to absorb tough blows and bounce back even stronger. We all know what it's like to be on a great team with a great culture because it is enjoyable, rewarding, and they win. In *High Ten*, Martin reinforces all of these lessons and more through a story where two teams – one athletic and one business – grow from good to great by focusing on their culture.

While I was serving as the Commandant of Cadets at the United States Military Academy, our primary and enduring focus was on developing leaders of character. For any future leader, there's much to learn in this book, from appreciating why people are the centerpiece of your culture to ways to empower your people and reap the value of their initiative to understanding and leveraging the "3 Bs" of culture – Beings (who we are), Beliefs (what we stand for), and Behaviors (how we do it) – and, finally, to recognizing the indicators of good culture. Leaders will also learn the significance of "Culture Crusaders," who perpetuate the culture, and to deeply examine their "Culture Custodians," coveting the "Culture Keepers" and rooting out the "Culture Vultures." As I read this book, I highlighted numerous passages, took notes, and reflected on my own efforts at creating cultures over the last 28 years of service. You can never stop studying leadership; it's a lifelong journey of education, experiences, and reflection.

Throughout *High Ten*, Martin also builds on his previous book, *Coach to Coach*, and reinforces that great leaders must also see themselves as coaches. He shares important insights on how to coach but also explains how a coach gets the whole team to steward the culture. It starts with the coach setting the foundation – the vision, standards, and expectations – and doing it alongside the players to maximize their ownership. Coaches then focus relentlessly on driving the team to achieve these goals.

Martin also subtly reinforces that leadership and coaching are more art than science. The Xs and Os and tactics matter, but he reminds us that ultimately it's the culture that determines success. As Martin writes, "Your competitive advantage is culture." If you want to learn to be a great coach and how to develop a great culture, then this book is for you!

Brigadier General Curtis A. Buzzard, U.S. Army

The views expressed in the foreword are those of the author and do not reflect the official position of the United States Military Academy, Department of the Army, or Department of Defense.

Introduction

In today's war for attention, culture is not simply a buzz-word. It's your biggest competitive advantage.

Before you worry about building your next program, product, or membership base, be more concerned with building a great culture first. As businesses and organizations learned during the pandemic, when you have a great culture, you are more prepared for big challenges. When you don't, you must be prepared to have more of them.

Everyone wants to feel both appreciated and part of something bigger – to feel part of a cool culture. The way a leader creates this special environment is by creating a culture based in trust, purpose, and fun.

But you may have heard that "culture isn't taught, it's caught."

High Ten is going to fly in the face of that statement and teach you about culture.

As you will learn, you don't get the culture for which you hope, wait, or wish – you get the one you design, implement, and maintain. And beware – if you don't design your culture, someone else will!

This book is the sequel to *Coach to Coach*. That book contained my philosophy of how to be a great coach and leader. In *High Ten*, I build on that information and teach you how a coach creates and leads a great culture. If you liked the easy-to-read style of *Coach to Coach*, you will enjoy following the journeys of Brian Knight and Marcus Chase 25 years later. Among all the positive feedback about *Coach to Coach*, the only critique was that the readers wanted more – more depth into the characters, more lessons, and more stories. I believe this book has made good on those requests.

High Ten is a business book, a sports book, and a motivational leadership book too. Although *High Ten* is a fictional story, the contents of this book are not theory; the information inside was produced through decades of real-life trial and error. Having helped build the cultures of two global businesses that have lasted a combined 40 years, this book was written so you enjoy the same success without making the same mistakes. Everything I have learned about culture from working with top professional and college sport teams, military organizations, and Fortune 500 companies is waiting for you inside.

To be clear, building or changing a culture can be difficult. Whether you are starting a business or already leading a company, team, or family, *High Ten* provides you with a working roadmap of how to navigate your current cultural challenges. Culture is not a one-time event; it's a never-ending process. And *High Ten* is your blueprint of how to build a culture that not only stands for something, but also stands the test of time. The question is not whether the culture lessons inside this book work, but whether you will work them. As any culture coach will tell you – what you permit, you promote.

In addition to helping you learn about people, *High Ten* will also teach you that there is no culture without communication. Do you have a team, leadership, or culture question? Do you have a favorite story or idea from either book? Write me at Martin@CoachingGreatness.com, and I look forward to starting a conversation.

I hope that you enjoy this book and, like Brian, Sam, and Marcus, that you never look at culture the same way again.

Giving you a big "High Ten,"

Martin Rooney
Gatlinburg, TN
2021

1

Trackside Diner

"Sorry it's taken so long to get together, Coach. Great to see you," said Marcus.

"Come on, kid," responded Brian, "after your big professional career and now becoming the youngest head coach at this prestigious school, I should thank you."

"Yeah right! As for 'youngest,' I'm feeling my age. And without you, this wouldn't be possible."

"Don't go soft on me," Brian said. "You've got work ahead bringing this place back to glory . . . and trying to unseat me as the best head coach this place ever had."

"Whoa!" exclaimed Marcus. "Is that what you call yourself? You know there've been legends here?"

"I know. I didn't want you to think rebuilding this program's gonna be easy. You're inheriting a losing program, and you aren't just inheriting the previous players – you're inheriting the previous problems too."

"Thanks for the reminder," Marcus said.

"Remember, Marcus, that's what coaches do. Sometimes it's a pat on the back and sometimes it's a kick in the pants. How's the move been?"

"Liz was nervous, but between my pro career and coaching, this's our fifth move in 24 years. She's knows how it works. The kids are resilient, and actually excited, which made the decision easier."

"That's great, and I can't wait to see them. Now the big question. How're you feeling?" Brian asked as he took another swig of beer.

"Well, coaching at my alma mater's a dream come true – and the big salary. But honestly, I'm scared. It's my first head job, and along with not feeling prepared, I feel pressured to win. It's not that the president and alumni aren't supportive, but I'm afraid to fail."

"That fear's a good thing," said Brian. "Means you care. Beware of when you don't care anymore. That's when you'll wish for something to put fear in your gut."

As Marcus listened, he realized his old coach was on his second beer. And that he'd been monopolizing the conversation.

"How've you been, Coach? What've you been up to?"

"Well," Brian sighed, "not much. After Kelly passed and I got her things in order, I never got started again. The kids visit, but they've got their own lives in other places. We'll be together over the holidays, but – I miss her so much."

"She was the best," said Marcus.

"Yeah, she was, kid," Brian said as he took another swig. "Enough of that. This's a reunion and new chapter for you. Have you met the team? What're your biggest challenges?"

Marcus answered, "I haven't met with them yet, since I need to get my coaching staff secured first. I'll let some old staff go, but a few match my style."

"And that style is?"

"You know me, Coach," smiled Marcus. "Like you, I love to fire people up with passion."

"I know you," laughed Brian. "Just wanted to make sure you did. That'll be important during this process. It'll be tough to stay who you are. Especially in the beginning."

"That's why you'll be my most important staff member, Coach."

"Is this a paid position?" Brian teased.

"Paid? You have money," laughed Marcus. "You want the job or what?"

"I don't know. I'm pretty busy," replied Brian. "What's the job title?"

"We could call you 'coach of the head coach.' Seriously, I need your help. You've forgotten more things about coaching than I'll ever know. Wouldn't you want to help this place win again?"

"You have good points . . . especially me knowing more than you . . . and I do like the title . . ." deliberated Brian.

"Come on. Don't do this to me. Just like your judo story, I need help making my weaknesses into strengths."

"Jeez, you remember that one, huh?" said Brian.

"I remember them all. You got me started in coaching, so this's all your fault," Marcus said. "Let's do this together. If we pull this off, there might be a shirt in it for you."

"Hmmm, I do like free gear. Okay kid, I'm in. Let's turn that fear into fun."

As Brian and Marcus ate, they talked about Marcus's decade playing in the pros, his family, and future ideas for his program. As Brian offered his coaching wisdom, Marcus noticed his old coach downed a few more beers. The rhythm of Brian and the waiter told Marcus that it wasn't Brian's first time drinking at Trackside.

Brian paid the tab without Marcus seeing it. His old coach still had some moves left.

As they put on their winter jackets, Brian said, "Say hi to Elizabeth and the kids. See you at my old – I mean, your new office next week?"

"Yes, Coach."

"And Marcus . . . *I am proud of you.*"

When he said those words, Marcus hugged Brian and whispered, "Thanks, Coach."

At that moment, Brian had a moment of déjà vu. At the same table where he met his mysterious old coach years before was seated a man with his head in his hands.

As Marcus headed out the door, Brian walked toward the table.

"Excuse me, do you need any help?" Brian asked.

"Can I have a tuna melt?" said the man.

Brian laughed and said, "Not that kind of help. I don't work here. But I recognize that look."

"What look?"

"That look when you have a problem and don't know how to fix it," said Brian.

The man looked away and said, "Nah, I'm good. I can handle it, thanks."

"With a tuna melt?"

"No, a tuna melt isn't going to fix this problem," said the man, smiling back. "This one requires a bacon double cheeseburger. . . ."

"That bad, huh? I know the feeling. I used to sit in that same seat when I had issues."

After a long pause as he wondered if the old man would go away, he asked, "If you don't work here, what do you do?"

"I'm retired, but I used to help people fix their problems by helping them get where they wanted to go. People called me a consultant," answered Brian.

"Ahh, I own a tech startup and we've had our share of consultants. Good gig if you ask me. You tell people ideas and if they work, you look great. If they fail, you say they didn't do them right," the man replied.

Brian paused as he pondered whether he should go away. Then he said, "To learn something new, sometimes you gotta read an old book, kid. I'm not sure if you're too proud or too afraid to ask for help."

Brian removed a gold-colored business card from his wallet. "Since I can't decide, here's my card."

The man read:

Brian Knight

Culture Coach

"Culture coach? I never heard that before," said the man.

"Most people haven't, kid. That's why so many businesses fail."

"Sorry I haven't been polite. It's been a tough day, and I don't usually meet people in diners."

"You should get out more," smiled Brian. "My name's Brian."

"I'm Sam . . . Sam Raucci."

"Nice to meet you, Sam, and good luck with your problem. If I were you, I'd stick with the tuna melt. First choices are often the right one."

"Thanks." Sam smiled.

"Before I go, I'll leave you with a question that always helped when I had troubles," offered Brian.

"Let's hear it," replied Sam.

"Ask yourself if you're unhappy about your dream come true."

As Sam processed the question, Brian called goodbye, to the Trackside staff and left.

Sam stared at the business card, and took the first of many pieces of Brian's advice and went with the tuna melt.

The race of life can do interesting things to people.

All three men drove home alone that night. One was scared because he knew what he had to do.

Another was stressed because he didn't have a clue. But the one who stopped off for a six-pack of beer didn't realize he was depressed because he thought he didn't have anything to do at all.

One race in the middle. One race starting. One race almost run.

Three heartbeats.

2

Make the Call

Sam awoke at 5:45 a.m. He didn't need an alarm clock because his stress woke him. By 6:05 he was showered, dressed, and out the door before his wife woke up. After a 20-minute commute, he arrived at his office. Sam liked being first to work because he felt safest in his office without having to talk to anyone. As he turned on his computer, he saw the business card that had been standing in between the keyboard keys for a week.

He picked up the card and thought, "How's an old man who still uses a business card going help a tech company?" Satisfied with his rationalization not to call, Sam returned the card and started working.

At 7:40, Sam was startled by a rare event: a knock at his door.

"Hi, Sam." Dana, the head of the customer service division, was looking distressed. "I know you're busy, but can we talk for a minute?"

"Uh, sure, Dana," replied Sam. "Come in."

Sam sat, but Dana remained standing. Before Sam could speak, Dana opened up.

"I'm sorry to tell you this, but a few things have me upset. I should've said something sooner, but I didn't want to jeopardize my job."

Sam was stunned. Because of her show of emotion, he didn't know how to respond. Lucky for him, Dana wasn't finished talking.

"When I came to Stamina, I was quiet. But my work here brought me out of my shell. A few days ago, at a meeting, Rick belittled me in front of everyone. I know you're good friends, and Rick's okay as a person. I'm upset because he and a number of people here don't take Stamina seriously. People just don't care. And there's always arguments because we're all on different pages."

"What do you mean?" asked Sam.

"Well, for one, Rick and his sales team sell features we don't have. They'll tell a customer anything to get a deal, and I'm left looking bad when I can't support something we don't offer. And his team doesn't respect the office. I keep cleaning up the conference room and that's not my job," answered Dana. "When I tell the engineers the new ideas customers want, they blow me off saying, 'That's impossible' or 'You don't understand.' And when our remote staff conferences in, most don't turn on their cameras. It's depressing that nobody seems excited about Stamina."

"I'm glad you're sharing this," said Sam, trying to utilize techniques from a leadership class. "And I'm sorry you feel this way."

That sentence didn't work how Sam intended.

"The final thing's the extra work you give me, Sam. I've made myself accessible at all times. When you fire out ideas to the group, I feel pressured to respond. It's too much. When I came on board, everyone was excited about 'Powering the people who power businesses.' But that feeling's gone. I wanted to share my feelings, and I also want to give my 30-day notice. I've grown here, but this isn't the place for me anymore. . . ." Dana finally broke down.

This upset Sam, and like many things lately, he didn't know what to do. Until that moment, Sam hadn't noticed Dana's value or how much she cared. He didn't want her to quit.

"Dana," Sam began, "I appreciate you talking to me about this. It's not your fault. I agree things've changed, but before you resign, let me try to fix things. You crying isn't a sign of weakness – it shows how much you care. You're valuable to Stamina and I would hate to see you leave."

Dana composed herself and said, "Thanks for listening. I want to stay, but I'm unsure anything will change. I'm sorry."

"No, Dana, I'm the one who's sorry. Thanks for caring about Stamina."

Dana smiled, nodded, and left.

When Sam closed his door, the safety of his office was gone. He couldn't lose Dana after the latest capital raise. The only person he confided in was Rick, but this problem concerned him. Instead of debating whether to call the number on the card, he debated whether 8 a.m. was too early to call a stranger. Sam called.

"Hello, this is Brian Knight," answered the voice.

"Oh, hey Mr. Knight. This is Sam Raucci . . . we met at Trackside last week?"

"Yes, of course Sam. And please . . . call me Brian. Mr. Knight's my father."

"Yes sir . . . I mean Brian. Is this an okay time to talk?"

"Sure, I've got time. I thought I'd hear from you. The way you looked the other night, you took longer than I expected."

"Well," Sam offered, "I took time thinking about the answer to your question, and I realized I'm unhappy about my dream come true."

"How so?"

"When we met, I'd just lost a dream deal with the university," said Sam. "Now I might lose a dream staff member too. And the dream raise for what everyone calls my dream business has me down."

"I see. You'll learn that deals, money, and people'll come and go. Dealing with them when they happen is the secret," said Brian.

Sam asked, "I've been wondering, what did you do as a consultant?"

"Well, I'd usually start with finding out everything about a company, and then observe the company in action. Once I knew how a business operated, I'd present my findings and suggestions how to fix what was broken."

"And the company would fix its problems?" asked Sam.

"Not always," said Brian. "I'd often set up ongoing consulting to assess progress and give them more action items."

"Could you help a business like mine?"

"I don't know," replied Brian with a laugh. "You haven't told me about your business yet!"

Sam spent 10 minutes covering Stamina's history as a sales and training company and its game-based software. Sam described Stamina's three capital raises since growing the business from a "side hustle" to a multimillion-dollar business. He shared about the pressure from his 30 employees, investors, and board of directors. Sam ended with his disconnection from the staff and how the recent holiday party was a disaster.

After Sam finished, Brian said, "Thanks for the information. It takes guts to admit your problems. Be proud of that. Can I give a couple first impressions?"

"Sure."

"First off, stop worrying about the past. That holiday party is ancient history like the Boston Tea Party. Second, you need to adjust how your company treats its people. Your customer service person's a star and you can't lose her."

"No, I can't," Sam confirmed.

"If you want to stop letting the past hold you hostage and improve in the future, then you must work on your *greatest competitive advantage* in the present," continued Brian.

"Our tech?"

"No!" answered Brian. "You've already learned your product can be great and your business can still suffer. There are plenty of businesses with plenty of products and startup cash that fail. Your competitive advantage is *culture*."

"Like the cultural differences of my staff?" asked Sam.

"Not entirely, but that's part of it. Culture goes beyond your country or ethnic background. Culture's everywhere. Cultures exist in sport teams and in businesses. Culture isn't a corporate buzzword; it's woven into everything your business does and is," explained Brian. "What I've learned so far is that Stamina's in trouble because you focused more on the architecture of your office than the architecture of your culture."

"I understand," said Sam. "There's a different feeling at work now. I wouldn't say negative, but distant. Is that what you mean?"

"That's another part of your culture," replied Brian. "It's a feeling, but it's also something others experience using your business. And this experience is created by the actions of the people who work there. When the culture's great, people are enthusiastic. With a culture like that, the customer feels it too. So your business is like an orange. When it gets squeezed, culture is the juice that comes out. If you don't like the taste, it's time to change the juice."

"That makes sense," said Sam. "But how do I know if I have a culture? It's not something I've covered with my team."

"You have a culture whether you like it or not. And the biggest mistake is not to design the culture you want. If you don't design Stamina's culture, someone else will. And when culture's treated like an afterthought, trouble follows closely behind. Now that it's caught up with you, it's easy to recognize."

"Got any quick suggestions?"

"There aren't 'quick fixes' because developing culture's a long process," answered Brian. "I have a lesson from my grandfather. He was a boxer. While fighting in a tournament, he won his first three fights, and before the final round of the final, his coach saw he was tired. The coach leaned over the ropes and yelled, 'This isn't the end of the fight. *It's the beginning!*'"

"I understand. So what can I do?"

"I have one suggestion."

"I'm all ears," replied Sam.

"Stop '*owning*' your company."

"What do you mean?"

"When we met," replied Brian, "you said you 'own' Stamina. As CEO, your job isn't to *own* Stamina, it's to *lead* it. You're the leader, so the culture is your responsibility. And getting your culture right will produce your most valuable asset – *ownership* by your people! Your job isn't creating software. It's creating your culture first. Problems have happened because it's the last thing on your mind."

"You're right," said Sam. "I haven't been a leader. And I definitely haven't designed the culture I'd like to have. Thanks. This really helped."

"Would you like to meet about culture?" asked Brian.

"You bet!"

"Good. Meet me at Arthur's this Friday at 9 a.m. You know the place?"

"Who doesn't?" replied Sam.

"Exactly," said Brian, "and I won't waste your time. Investing in culture will be your best investment."

"I wanna be up front," said Sam. "As for investing, we don't have a budget for consulting."

"Don't worry about money . . . you can afford my coffee and bagel, right?"

"Yeah, I can cover that," laughed Sam.

"Then you got yourself a culture coach, kid."

3

Brick Walls

As Brian walked the campus, different landmarks acted as muses. A statue reminded him of the day he got the head coaching job. The auditorium prompted thoughts of the days when his girls had graduated. The lakeside bench where Kelly would meet him for lunch made him wonder if she waited on a bench for him somewhere. Memory Lane ended at the stadium. After climbing the stairs, he smiled at the newly placed placard on his old office:

Marcus Chase

Head Football Coach

"Knock, knock," called Brian. "Is the new head coach around?"

"Hey, Coach!" exclaimed Marcus seated at his desk. "He's around, but he should be out recruiting."

As Brian removed his coat, he examined the new look of his old office.

Marcus said, "Glad you're here, Coach. You're the first to see. What do you think?"

Brian silently looked at photos, trophies, and rings from Marcus's career as a player and coach. The walls were filled with an impressive collection of his football history.

"Looks like you wanna be somewhere else."

"What?" Marcus answered in surprise. "I put a lot of time into this."

"I'm sure – and more time into attaining these accomplishments. But how you've set up this room won't set up your team to win. Lemme sit down before you get worked up. I've got a present that'll help."

Brian sat, opened his bag, and removed an object.

"Merry Christmas, kid," Brian said as he placed a gold-painted brick on Marcus's desk.

"What's with the brick?"

"It's not what's with it," answered Brian. "It's what's on it. A brick's a brick. But this one's special. It was given to me when I got my first head coaching job. Now I'm giving it to you."

"Is it a doorstop?"

"It's not a stop, it's a start. This brick's the cornerstone of what you'll build here. I brought this brick to remind you of two important questions, but after seeing your office, you'll have three questions to answer to turn this team around. Pick up the brick and I'll give you those questions."

"Do I have to hold it?" smiled Marcus.

"Indulge me."

Marcus reluctantly picked up the golden brick and Brian continued, "Now you're ready. The first question is, 'Am I knocking down the brick walls my players and coaches have built around themselves?' And the second is, 'Am I the coach my people would run through a brick wall for?'"

Marcus realized the challenges ahead.

Brian continued, "This brick's to remind you before you build a strong offense here that it's more important to build strong *relationships*. Without them, your team'll be challenged to win, even with great players. To build those relationships, you'll need a special kind of glue. And that glue's what the third question's about."

"I hear you," replied Marcus, recognizing that aside from press conferences and a few introductions, he didn't know anyone there. "You're earning your

T-shirt. The brick and questions are useful. What's the third one?"

"I only used those two questions when I coached. But after touring the 'Marcus Chase Memorial,' there's one more question you must ask before the other two. If you don't get that answer right, the other answers don't matter."

"The Marcus Chase Memorial? Ha! What's the question?"

"Okay," replied Brian. "The third question is, 'Am I the best representative of our culture?'"

"What's that mean?"

"Look at the walls," Brian began. "It's obvious you were a great football player. And this stuff proves you're a football coach too. But it's time to be a great culture coach. Like coaching requires you to be more excited about someone else than yourself, this job requires you to be more excited about your culture than yourself. Look around. I see you and your history, but one thing's sure. . . . I don't see much about the culture you want. Especially the colors. If that brick's gonna be the cornerstone of your culture, everything in this room should be built upon it and match. I'm not saying this stuff isn't cool, but it should be in your home."

"Does everything have to go?"

"No," Brian replied. "Some things like the team photos and bowl ring when you played here are great. They're part of your connection to this school. But most of this stuff doesn't connect. That's not why kids'll want to come here. A head coach can't look confused where he is . . . or where he wants to be."

"I feel you, Coach," sighed Marcus. "I'm proud of that stuff and wanted everyone to know about me.

But you're right. It's not about me, it's about the culture for them."

"Correct," beamed Brian. "And don't forget one more thing about culture. . . ."

"What's that?"

"It isn't just the culture you create *for* them. Yes, your culture has to be deliberate, but for it to be something they want to belong to, you'll have to create parts of it *with* them too."

Marcus scanned the room. "Thanks, Coach. Looks like I've gotta change the color scheme, huh?"

"It's not just the colors you see. Culture begins with the way you see yourself. Until you see yourself as a culture coach more than a former player, you won't coach for culture. Remember, the culture must flow through your veins before it will flow through your team. If you cut your wrist, it should bleed gold and blue."

Marcus stared at the brick.

"Yeah," said Brian, "people will measure your program according to the 'buy-in' of your team. That's a culture paradox, because buy-in never happens without the leader taking ownership first. Ownership's demonstrated by everything you do. Down to the colors of these walls."

"Geez," said Marcus. "Would've been easier to stay defensive coordinator."

"Yes, it would," Brian replied. "You're gonna learn there's a big difference between playing an instrument and being the conductor. As a player or a defensive coach, you only worried about a couple of positions. Now you must worry about all of them. And don't forget the conductor's got his back to the crowd because it's not about him – it's about them."

Marcus nodded.

"You're ready to be head coach," Brian continued. "You're now one of the most important people at this school. Football generates money for the university and other sports, and brings in fans and future students. You'll have more responsibilities, and some of them aren't enjoyable. Everyone besides you will look at things through a straw, only seeing the area for which they're responsible. But the head coach sees *everything*. Before, as assistant coach, you didn't care as much about team GPA or ticket sales. But now, in addition to coaching, you must build your staff and recruit with media engagements and fundraising thrown in too."

"Ugh, sounds like a lot of work."

"That's why the head coach gets the big bucks," smiled Brian. "Don't forget your job description is summarized with three letters: W-I-N. Regardless of the players you recruit and the coaches you hire, it's harder to win without a confident head coach. That confidence happens when everyone's connected to the culture. Culture, like building a winning football team, doesn't happen overnight. And culture's hard to create – and even harder to change. That's why your first assignment, besides redoing this office, is deciding what to *write* on that brick!"

"You lost me." Marcus smiled.

"Some teams call it a motto. Others a mantra or a slogan. I'm sure your past teams had them. But I'm talking about more than a cool quote. I want you to write an easy-to-understand summary of your culture so your team knows what it stands for . . . and they stand for it."

"I understand, Coach," said Marcus. "I have some favorites and was thinking of bringing back Coach Olsen's 'Hold the Rope' motto. That one always worked."

"Nah. Sounds like 'Grandma's ham.'"

"Grandma's ham?" inquired Marcus.

"You'll like this," Brian began. "One holiday dinner a woman was cooking ham. Before she put it in the oven, she cut off 25% of the ham and threw it away. Her young daughter was watching and asked, 'Mom, why'd you throw away part of the ham?' Her mother said, 'That's how your grandma did it and her ham was so good, I cut off the end too.' The little girl said, 'Grandma's here, so let's ask her.' They asked her grandmother why she removed that portion of the ham. Her grandmother said, 'That's how my mother did it and her ham was so good, I cut off the end too.' As luck would have it, the little girl's 89-year-old great-grandmother was not only alive, but there too! So the little girl asked her, 'Nana, can you tell me why cutting off the end of the ham made your ham so good?' And she said, 'Child, it had nothing to do with making it good. I cut off the end because my oven was so small, it was the only way it would fit!'"

"Another classic," said Marcus smiling.

"Know this," replied Brian, "using people's old stuff might not make sense to a new generation. Yes, 'Hold the Rope' was cool, but that's Grandma's ham. This is your first team. The slogan needs to be yours too."

"I appreciate that . . . and it's gonna be more work."

"It's work that'll do work for you," replied Brian. "The motto you write on that brick will guide your team. It should direct the team's behavior so you can spend less time 'policing' and more time building. I want you to create something special."

"Roger, Coach. I won't let you down."

"I know you won't, Marcus. You've always been my greatest student. And that's why you can handle one more idea. I've been thinking about what separated my greatest teams from the less successful. It wasn't talent level. Now don't get me wrong – it's difficult to win without talent, and that's why recruiting's important. But some years I won with talented players and some years I lost. In addition to this office and working on the motto, you need to start mixing the cement that'll hold this team together."

"With all this painting and mixing, I should've gone into construction," laughed Marcus.

"That's not as crazy as it sounds. Culture is always under construction." Brian grinned. "Can I explain the cement, or what?"

"Yes, Coach."

"Good," smiled Brian. "When I stopped coaching, I started consulting for teams and businesses. As my jobs increased, so did my time on airplanes. Spending so much time on planes got me used to delays, connections, and even airplane food. But one thing that never got easier was turbulence. One flight taught me an important lesson. From the moment I heard, 'Flight attendants, take your jump seats!' things got ugly. The plane was bouncing so much, I gripped the handrests in fear. I thought I was handling it well, but then I saw a young girl sitting calmly in her seat. About 10 years old. I was amazed by her composure. She stayed more relaxed than anyone on the plane, including a veteran of the skies like myself. We finally passed the storm and eventually landed. I wanted her secret to staying calm. She waited for the passengers to disembark, so I waited too. Then I said, 'Miss, the way you stayed so calm on the flight was inspiring. What's your secret?' The little girl looked up and said, 'Sir, there's no secret. My father's the pilot and he said we were going home. I stayed calm *because I trust him*.'"

"Great story."

"Your culture's cement is 'Trust.' My greatest teams had it and my worst ones didn't. So, as the pilot of this team, when you create your motto for the brick, I want you to make sure it doesn't just inspire, but it builds trust too. After all, that's what 'run through a brick wall for you' means – trusting someone so much you'd attempt the impossible."

"I trust you, Coach," said Marcus.

"That's the spirit," said Brian. "Don't forget when you meet with them, meet them where they are, not where you want them to be. Building trust starts there."

"Roger that. Speaking of trust, there's one thing you can do for me."

"Already giving out orders, huh?" laughed Brian.

"Not an order, just a request, Coach. I don't know all the rules of my culture yet, but I know one of them will be no alcohol. Since I consider you part of my team, I want to know if you're on board with that."

After a pause, Brian responded, "I can do it...Coach."

Both men were ready to try something different. For Marcus, it was a team motto. For Brian, it was a six-pack of seltzer.

4

Arthur's Bagels

Amid the buzz of Arthur's patrons enjoying their breakfast, Sam scanned the busy seating section and thought, "Maybe he isn't coming." Then he noticed someone waving with both arms in the back corner. That someone was Brian.

"Hey Brian," said Sam, sitting down. "Good to see you again, and thanks for meeting. Been here long?"

"Only a few minutes," replied Brian. "I've learned that if you're on time, you're already late for something."

Sam scanned the restaurant. "I haven't been here in a while. This place hasn't changed a bit. It was one of my favorite haunts."

"Me too. So you went to school here?"

"Yes. My friends and I used this place as a study hall, but Arthur's coffee also saved me after many a late night," laughed Sam. "Should we order or is this just a meeting?"

"Actually," smiled Brian, "my first lesson's about why we *must* order. If I wanted to have 'just a meeting,' it would've been somewhere quieter. We're here to *break bread.*"

"You made a good choice. Few bagels better than Arthur's."

"You'll see," hinted Brian, "why you're so fond of this place has less to do with the bagels than you think. Breaking bread isn't only about food. It's about building relationships. When people enjoy a meal together, guards come down and communication goes up. I don't know the science, but meals make connections stronger."

Sam pulled out his phone and started typing "break bread." He said, "I hope you don't mind, I want to take notes on your ideas."

"I don't mind notes at all. They show you're a good student and value the information. What I do mind is how you take them. It seems 'old school,' but I brought something for you."

Brian pulled out a gold-colored notebook and slid it to Sam.

"What's this?" asked Sam.

"That could be the most important business book you ever own."

Sam flipped through the pages.

"But there's nothing inside? Lemme guess; it'll be my most important business book after I fill it with your lessons, right?"

"Bingo, kid. Call me old-fashioned, but I believe writing notes is better than typing on your phone. Once you 'think it and ink it,' you've made that idea more real."

"I didn't bring a pen," said Sam, frowning.

Brian reached into his coat pocket and produced a pen like a magician pulling a rabbit from a hat.

"Voilà! I've always got pens with me. My old coach said to have a pen and paper because your mind might forget, but the paper would always remember. Now," said Brian pointing at the book, "when you said there was nothing inside, that wasn't true. One of the pages isn't blank."

On his second pass, Sam still found nothing.

"Okay, what's the trick?"

"No trick, Sam," Brian said opening it to the first page. "It's the next lesson: culture's hard to see if you don't know where to look. What's on that first page?"

"Well, I do see that tiny dot."

"And what else?" quizzed Brian.

"I see it's blue?"

"And?"

"Nothing?" offered Sam.

"That's what most people see, Sam. Especially with culture."

"A blue dot? I don't get it."

"The blue dot represents the 'little troubles' bringing you down – your problem with Dana or the deal you missed. It can also represent the minutia of the products Stamina produces," said Brian. "You see those dots every day. But what people can't see is all the white space that surrounds the dots in our lives. We get so focused on the dot, we forget the white space. The culture of your business is that white space, and like most leaders, to you it's invisible. And when something's invisible, it gets no attention."

Sam nodded.

"As your culture coach," continued Brian, "my goal is to help you see things you never saw before. Because I'm 'old school,' I can't change the dots in your life. But I can help you change your culture surrounding those dots."

"I won't forget that one."

"Let's not forget to break bread, either," smiled Brian. "Before your next lesson, you owe me a bagel and coffee. So get me an everything bagel and a latte."

While standing in line, Sam thought about the blue dots in his life, and felt hopeful Brian could help with them. He returned with their food.

"Here you go. You didn't say what size latte, so I went with the biggest."

"Good move, kid. Can't go wrong with overdelivering, right? Now, for your first quiz as a cultural apprentice. What did you see in line?"

"What do you mean?" asked Sam.

"You said you've been here many times. So, tell me about the culture of Arthur's."

"You're talking about the white spaces, right?"

"Yes," replied Brian. "Tell me something you saw and how it made you feel."

Sam thought and said, "One thing was how the girl behind the counter knew the first name of the person in front of me. That was cool. And the way everyone was smiling and said 'thank you' made me feel good."

"Nice," said Brian. "Anything else?"

"Something that made Arthur's special to me was ordering a half dozen bagels and having the server throw in an extra one. Like our little secret or something. I loved that about this place and I saw they're still doing it."

"After all your visits, that was your first view of Arthur's 'white spaces,'" smiled Brian proudly. "Don't worry, you'll get better at it. Like gravity, culture isn't something you see. It's something you *feel*. Culture's like your business's life force, and just like a life force makes the grass and your hair grow, the culture can make your business grow too."

Sam took a note in his golden notebook.

"Whoa," sighed Sam. "That was deep. Is culture tough to implement?"

"Don't worry, kid. Culture can seem complex, but I'm going to break it into simple pieces for you. Over years of teaching culture, I've learned not to overwhelm people."

"Thanks," said Sam. "You're a great teacher. Where do we start?"

"We start with the first of the three Bs of culture . . . *Beings*."

Sam wrote the word.

"Since you're aware every business has a culture, you're ready to learn the three things that determine how a culture looks, acts, and feels. What you mentioned about Arthur's wasn't about the bagels – it was about the *people*! Simply put, you can't have a culture without people. So, before a business concerns itself with 'what we make,' it should focus on '*who we are*.'"

"Makes sense," said Sam. "Does having the right people always lead to a great culture?"

"No. Creating a great culture would be easy if it wasn't for the people!" said Brian with a laugh. "You need great people, but getting those people to create a great culture takes work. You must understand your people are the centerpiece of your culture – and those people fall into one of two categories."

Sam bulleted the numbers.

"The first category is *Culture Crusaders*," Brian explained. "These people are the ones who not only determine the culture they want, but are also tireless champions of that culture. As CEO, you must be a Crusader. It's your responsibility to create and uphold the culture at Stamina. Most leaders, unfortunately, are taught less about culture and more about delegating. The one thing a leader should never delegate is their culture. But this happens all the time."

Sam said. "That stings. I haven't been much of a Crusader."

"That's okay, kid. That's why you're here. Since I've convinced you to stop 'owning" Stamina and start 'leading' it, it's up to you to set the culture and embed it into your business. Embedding your culture starts with Crusaders, but maintaining that culture relies on the second category of Beings: your *Culture Custodians*."

As Sam took notes, he said, "When I hear 'custodian' I remember high school. Custodian was a fancy name for 'janitor.' Does this next group deal with taking out the garbage?"

"Not exactly, but you'll learn one subgroup of Culture Custodians don't take out the garbage, they feed off it! Although the word 'custodian' can refer to a person who cleans a building, I use a different definition – a custodian's someone who has a responsibility to look after someone or something. A Culture Custodian is responsible for looking after your culture."

"Got you," said Sam. "So the Culture Custodians look after and uphold the culture the Crusader has created?"

"In a perfect world, yes. But perfect cultures would be easy if it wasn't for the people! The word 'custodian' isn't positive or negative. It means they've been given authority over your culture. How they use that authority's another matter. That's why there are two subgroups of Culture Custodians. One of them strengthens culture and the other destroys it. The first subgroup is your *Culture Keepers* and the second's your *Culture Vultures*."

"Keepers, huh?" said Sam. "Sounds like a big fish."

"Yup," smiled Brian. "The word's used for partners too – 'she's a keeper.' You're on the right track because your Culture Keepers are Beings you don't wanna let go. A keeper's defined as a person who manages something for someone. The difference from being a neutral 'custodian' is that a Keeper's expected to 'keep' the culture better than the leader left it. If you think about a zookeeper, they're expected to make the zoo a better place, not worse. Or from sports, imagine a goalkeeper. That keeper minds the net he's responsible for, and attempts to prevent bad things from happening."

"I understand," said Sam "As we're covering these, I'm already categorizing my staff."

"That's natural," replied Brian, "and something a leader should do. Each Keeper's ability to uphold your culture is different, but to be categorized a keeper, they should at least maintain the culture you want. Before you get excited figuring how many 'Keepers' you've got, let's worry about another animal at the zoo. As much as Keepers help your business, Culture Vultures do damage."

"Let me guess," interrupted Sam. "They feed off the garbage?"

"Yes! A vulture's a scavenging bird of prey that feeds off carrion – decaying flesh of animals. You might be familiar with vultures because they're often depicted circling above people in distress."

"That's how I picture them. They're ugly!'

"Ugly for your business. If you've seen vultures, they're never alone either. Vultures gather and interestingly, a group of them sitting together is called a 'committee,' while a group of them feeding's called a 'wake.' So you're right about the garbage. The Culture Vultures not only love to feed off the bad news and negative aspects of your business, but they also gather in committees to enjoy what's rotten."

"Ugh," grunted Sam. "I've placed some staff in this category, and one of those placements hurts. Can your business survive with a bunch of Vultures?"

"Sorry, kid. That ends up with a wake."

Sam reviewed his notes. "This morning's been more insightful than I hoped. I had my doubts, but you've made me a believer. Any chance we can work together? I know you can help Stamina get on track."

"Thanks, Sam. It's my pleasure to share these lessons. For me to best help you and Stamina, we'll need more than one-on-one meetings. I'm recommending my *Cultural Checkup*."

"What's that?" asked Sam. "Checkups remind me of my doctor."

Brian chuckled. "You're not far off. But instead of your health, imagine the Culture Checkup's an examination of Stamina's health. Many people ignore the health of their business until there's a problem. With my checkup, your business won't get sicker before it gets better. How it works is I meet with you individually for three mornings to teach more about culture. Then I meet with your staff, and do a 'walk-through' around Stamina. At the end of the three days, I'll share what I found and deliver a treatment plan. Sound good?"

"Sounds great . . . and expensive," sighed Sam. "Let's cut to the chase. What's this checkup cost?"

"That's the best part. Unlike visiting your doctor or mechanic, you decide what I'm worth *after* the checkup."

"Really?" asked Sam.

"Once we cover my diagnosis and treatment plan, you can decide whether to hire me as a consultant," Brian said. "So, do you want the checkup? What've you got to lose?"

Sam agreed and the men shook on it.

"Great work today," encouraged Brian. "Until we meet up, I want you doing two things in preparation. First, continue to categorize Stamina's Beings into either Crusaders, Keepers, or Vultures."

"Check."

"And second," said Brian, "get some new glasses . . ."

"What's wrong with my glasses?"

"No worries," replied Brian. "I mean I want you to use a new set of culture lenses. Think like X-ray vision, but instead of bones, they expose culture. Look at Stamina like you examined the 'white space' of Arthur's. Take detailed notes, and email what you find."

"Check," affirmed Sam.

"It's not as easy as it seems," said Brian as he flicked a coin toward Sam and said, "Catch!"

Sam caught it.

"What did I throw?"

Sam answered, "A dime."

"Good. Now close your hand around it. You seen a dime before?"

"Of course," replied Sam.

"Tell me who's on the front and which way he faces," said Brian.

"Uh . . ." Sam hesitated.

"Not sure? Okay, tell me the three items on the back."

Sam stood in silence.

"The man on the front's Franklin Roosevelt, and he faces left," said Brian. "On the back are an olive branch, torch, and oak branch, from left to right."

Sam opened his hand and confirmed it.

"I didn't do that to you to distress you," said Brian, "but to impress upon you there's a big difference between *looking* and *paying attention*. And last thing. The lenses also work at home. I know we haven't talked about it, but Stamina isn't the only place with 'white space' around the dots. Culture happens at home too."

5

New Lenses

"Can't believe we lost another five-star player," thought Marcus as he stared out his office window. Marcus had another late day at the stadium picking up the broken pieces of his program. Because the records for the last two seasons were 4 and 7 and 3 and 8, Marcus didn't have to guess he'd been hired to turn the program around; the president, athletic director, and boosters had made that crystal clear.

"The old man's right again," Marcus mumbled under his breath. He sat and looked over his schedule. Packed with recruiting trips, interviews, and meetings, it overwhelmed him. He picked up the golden brick.

"Am I doing anything to knock down the walls the previous players and staff have built around themselves?"

Marcus had held a team meeting to introduce himself before the holidays. He knew that after New Year's would be time to start building relationships with his players, but the former coaching staff wouldn't have to wait until after the holidays to learn where their job stood. Marcus had begun interviewing the previous coaches for their jobs.

"Am I the coach my people would run through a brick wall for?"

His answer was no. With few exposures and knowing relatively little about his players, Marcus was not the pilot of this team. Yes, he'd been a star in the NFL, but for these kids to trust him, he needed to connect with them. That connection would be made stronger when his team understood his philosophy. Marcus spun the brick and asked the third question.

"Am I the best representative of our culture?"

He answered by standing up and removing more items from the walls and shelves. While he rearranged his office for the second time that week, he thought about the motto he'd write on that brick.

That morning, Sam also followed his instructions. Instead of "business as usual," Sam attempted to see with a new set of lenses. Rather than rushing out and beating everyone to the office, Sam made himself waffles. As he ate, he opened his golden notebook and continued categorizing his staff as "Crusaders," "Keepers," and "Vultures."

"Morning, sunshine," said Melissa. "Forget to wake up today?"

"No, Meliss, I'm shaking things up. I'm going in late to see what Stamina does when I'm not there."

"Like they can do anything if you're not there. What are you working on?" she asked pointing at his notebook. "I didn't know that was your color."

"What? Shiny gold's my thing," Sam quipped. "You might not believe this, but I got this from someone I met at Trackside diner."

"In a diner?" said Melissa. "This isn't some religion thing, is it?"

"Noooo," smiled Sam. "He's a consultant who helps businesses work on their culture."

"Ohhh, got his number? The partners at Riley and Riley need it. That place is toxic."

"Still bad, huh?"

"And getting worse," replied Melissa. "Everyone's out to get each other. If you aren't by the watercooler, watch your back."

"Sounds like you've got 'vultures' over there. Circling the water cooler . . ."

"True," said Melissa. "That's more accurate than calling us 'ambulance chasers.'"

"You know what they say," said Sam baiting Melissa. "What'd you call a courteous person at a bar association convention?"

"What?"

"The caterer," laughed Sam.

"Okay, have a good day," she said grabbing her coffee. "I'll get ready for another day around those vultures."

"Good luck, Meliss, I know you can do it. You know what I say when someone finds out my wife's a lawyer . . ."

"What's that," rolling her eyes.

"They ask if living with a lawyer's tough. I say, 'Tough? Do you know the difference between my wife and a pit bull?' When they say, 'No," I answer, 'Her lipstick!'" said Sam running before the "stick" in lipstick left his lips. Melissa chased him to the door and kissed him goodbye for the first time in a while.

The good energy was short-lived. After entering Stamina's 7,000-square-foot office space, Sam's optimism vanished. Sam walked right to his office and closed the door. His golden notebook reminded him waffles weren't the only thing he'd do differently; he'd also search Stamina's "white space." Rather than start his computer, Sam looked around with new lenses.

The first thing Sam noticed was silence. In contrast to the hum of Arthur's, Stamina seemed more mausoleum than tech startup. He looked through the glass wall into the open area and saw a few people at desks throughout the room. In addition to the lack of noise, the room also lacked energy. With ear buds in and backs to each other, the employees of Stamina were in their own worlds.

Sam walked through the common area undetected. He passed blank flat-screen TVs that should've been playing the Stamina marketing loops, which had cost money and time. The TVs weren't the only things not serving their purpose; of their four "huddle" rooms meant to serve as meeting places, two were unused and two others had a sole employee inside. Sam walked to the cantina, an area meant to allow Stamina employees to clear their minds with the help of coffee or snacks. Sam heard voices, which gave him hope the common area wasn't a true reflection of Stamina's culture. But when he entered the cantina, his hope disappeared as fast as the discussion. Rick and two employees stared at Sam like they'd seen a ghost.

"Hey, Sammy," started Rick. "What're you doing 'round these parts?"

"Hey, Rick . . . Brandon and Lucas," replied Sam. "Yeah, I don't visit the cantina much anymore. I've decided to check in on everyone. What're you guys up to?"

"Ah, you know," replied Rick. "Going over sales stuff. You hear I got that minor league baseball team account?"

"Yes," answered Sam.

"Yeah, too bad you couldn't close the university deal," Rick said, as Brandon and Lucas picked up their coffee and walked past Sam.

Sam waited until they left. "Say, listen Ricky," he started. "We're working with a consultant on fixing the culture here, and I have to ask you . . . Did you have a run-in with Dana?"

"Ugh," Rick slumped. "Not another one of those marketing groups telling us how to do our business? And why? Did Dana say something? She's such a whiner. Always whining about what I should be doing. She's driving my sales team nuts."

"No, Rick. This isn't about marketing. It's about righting the ship. If you haven't noticed, Stamina's lost its mojo. I know you bring in sales, but Dana's responsible for serving the people you sell. She's gotten positive feedback from our accounts, so it'd help if you could work together."

"Change how I do things for her?" snapped Rick. Then he calmed himself and said, "Okay, buddy, I'll work on it. When are we getting dinner with the girls? It's been forever."

"I'll check with Melissa."

"Okay, keep me posted," said Rick as he slid past him.

Sam spent the next hour walking Stamina. He was proud of the workspace he'd helped design. But as he took notes on the "white space" of Stamina, that pride turned to shame. On the bright side, he enjoyed visiting Stamina's "lab." Since Sam was a self-proclaimed "tech nerd," he felt comfortable with the engineers and their technology. The Stamina engineers had the latest in everything, from ergonomic chairs to oversized dual-screen monitors.

Sam asked Dana to grab lunch. While eating, Dana opened up about the company, proving Brian's theory that people become more authentic when you break bread.

That Wednesday was uneventful for Brian. For the last year, he'd measured his days by his self-medication schedule: three coffees in the morning and six beers at night. The hours between doses were filled with reading or social media. Aside from the occasional errand, Brian had little to do. Now committed to seltzers, he was at the grocery store examining a 12-pack like a sommelier choosing a fine wine. While pulling a cranberry-essence box from the stack, his phone rang.

"Hello," answered Brian.

"Hey, Coach," said Marcus. "You up?"

"I'm talking aren't I? What's up?"

"Sorry it's late," began Marcus. "I'm still at the stadium. You'll be happy to know I'm fixing up my office."

"You calling about paint colors? That gold's tough to match," joked Brian.

"No, Coach. It's been a long week. Recruiting has me scrambling to put a class together, so I've been busy. I'm calling because I've been thinking about your three questions and need more help. The good news is we have the talent to win games and some solid coaches from last year's team. I'll make a few personnel changes, but the players or staff aren't the reason they're losing."

"What do you think it is?" asked Brian.

"I think they lost because they didn't have a winning culture."

"You could be on to something, kid," replied Brian. "What'll you do about it?"

"I was hoping you'd help me with that one. No one knows more about winning cultures than you."

"Well, you got me drinking these seltzers, the least I can do is help bring a national powerhouse back to prominence."

"Great!" said Marcus. "How 'bout we meet next Monday?"

"Monday's no good for me," Brian said.

Marcus waited for the punchline.

"Seriously, Marcus, I'm meeting with another group. How about Tuesday?"

"Okay, Coach," said Marcus. "Tuesday it is. How 'bout 7 a.m. at my office?"

"As long as it looks good this time, kid."

They hung up and Brian chose the lemon-essence seltzer. When Brian got home, he felt a spring in his step.

When he popped on his computer and the top of a seltzer, his inspiration increased with an email from Sam.

To: bknight@aol.com
Reply-To: sraucci@stamina.com
Subject: <u>"Beings" Update from Sam</u>

Brian,

I wanted to report in on Stamina's culture. I used my new lenses and searched for "white space." As expected, not everything was rainbows and unicorns.

I'm sad to say there isn't the collaboration or pride in the work I hoped to find. The separate divisions in the company are at odds with each other.

As for Stamina's Beings, my disconnection from many of them makes it difficult to categorize their custodian subtype. One excuse is some of my staff work remotely. I made rough guesses, and I can say with confidence there are more "keepers" than "vultures," but the birds of prey are circling.

You'd like that I broke bread with Dana, and the meeting was productive.

Finally, something you mentioned last week affected me. Of all my "Beings," I realize my wife is the most important. When I tried to categorize her at Stamina, I made the sad realization she isn't on the team.

I'm not sure if that's important or not, but wanted you to know.

I hope this info helps your check-up process. Looking forward to Monday!

Sam

Stamina – Powering the People Who Power Businesses

While Sam was waiting for Melissa to get home, he felt his phone vibrate. "The old guy's pretty quick," he thought as he opened his email.

To: sraucci@stamina.com
Reply-To: bknight@aol.com
Re: "Beings" Update from Sam

Sam,

Thanks for your update and your honesty.

A leader is required to show courage. You did that by admitting your challenges.

What you're experiencing isn't unique. Here's a little leadership tip: Stamina's always going to present new challenges. A great culture won't stop them from coming, but it will help weather the storm when they do.

The information about your wife is important. Your business is like your marriage: If you stop working on it, it stops working too.

I was married for 35 years. You're just beginning. The best way to think about your marriage is how you refer to Stamina: It's a "startup" too.

See you Monday.

Brian

6

The Checkup

Brian's GPS brought him to Stamina at 8:50 a.m. As he closed his car door, Sam walked down the sidewalk to meet him.

"You made it!" exclaimed Sam. "Any trouble finding this place?"

"No sir," replied Brian, "GPS made it easy. What a beautiful complex. I've driven past it for years, but never pulled in. I remember when they built this place."

"Ugh," smiled Sam. "Don't remind me. That build's one process I don't want to relive."

"That's exactly why I'm here! Instead of building an office, we'll be building your culture. The construction of this facility was painful, but don't forget how you liked the finished product. My job's to make that happen with your culture . . . with less pain."

Sam walked Brian into Stamina's headquarters. Like a proud parent, Sam showed him the office space. Sam introduced Brian to some staff members and explained their roles. After the tour, Sam led Brian to his office, and the lesson began.

"Like I said," Brian started. "Stamina's got a culture. That's for sure."

"Is it bad?" asked Sam.

"That's not what I mean. There's a culture here whether you designed it or not. When people get together, a culture develops. Whether it's "good" or "bad" is according to how far the culture is from the culture you want. But don't worry; the checkup will show us where you are. Then we can take the culture where you want it to go."

"Gotcha," replied Sam. "I'm unsure what I want, but I know this isn't it. Does that make sense?"

"Absolutely. Open your notebook . . . today's lesson will give you more clarity."

Sam opened his notebook and Brian began.

"At Arthur's, you learned the first B of culture, Beings. Remember, without people you can't have a culture. You also learned to place your Beings into three categories to identify where they stand. Where they stand concerns the second of B of culture. *Beliefs* are the *'what we stand for'* of your culture."

Sam took notes.

"So," Brian continued, "you don't have the culture you want because your Beings don't stand for your Beliefs! The problem isn't their fault – it's yours because you haven't made those Beliefs clear. Your job's to fill Stamina with good Beings, and fill them with the Beliefs you want them to embrace. If you don't, the culture won't match the one you want."

Sam wrote more notes. "You're right. They don't feel the same way about Stamina as I do, and I haven't done a good job getting them to see my beliefs. How can I do that?"

"Exactly!"

"What?" Sam asked. "Is this another test?"

"Not a test. Just letting you know you answered your question," Brian smirked.

"Come on . . . what is it?" asked Sam.

"You said you want to get your people to *see* your beliefs. Well . . . the way you do that is giving them your *vision*! You might've heard, 'Culture eats strategy for breakfast,' but that's only true after a leader shares a compelling enough vision to get that culture hungry to eat."

"Is this another lens lesson?"

"Close, because it deals with seeing things," replied Brian. "The lens idea had you on the 'lookout' for Stamina's current culture. A vision is your view of the future."

"You mean my vision for the company?"

"Yes, but your vision is the important Belief everyone at Stamina should share. Your vision should inspire anyone who comes into contact with Stamina. It should be the reason people want to work here. A great culture stands for the vision, but without one, a weak culture falls for anything."

Sam took notes and said, "When I started Stamina, I had a clear vision about sales training. We had a strong culture too. But with the capital raises, and new people and services, I'm not sure of my vision for Stamina anymore. And if I'm not sure, how can anyone else be?"

"Presto!" said Brian. "If the leader has no vision, everyone who works for him runs blind! That's why you must do the first of two important jobs concerning the Beliefs of your company. You must *envision the vision*. Only after you know and believe the vision will your staff also believe."

Sam asked, "What's the second thing to do for Stamina's Beliefs?"

"After you envision the vision, you give them a cultural compass. These are values that direct them while that vision's carried out. Once your people envision the vision, they must also *value the values*."

"I think I understand," said Sam. "If you noticed, Stamina's core values were posted out front."

"I did notice. But I've also noticed those values aren't being carried out by your Beings. If I saw them correctly, I think your three core values are 'Honesty, Positivity, and Excellence.'"

"Wow," answered Sam. "Great memory."

"It's not about my memory. How about your memory? And the memory of your Beings? Do you think they live according to those values, and use them as a compass toward your vision?"

"I guess not," shrugged Sam.

Brian said, "That's because values are rarely internally processed when they're externally processed."

Sam was confused. "What?"

"How'd you come up with those values?"

"Six years ago, I attended a leadership seminar, and after a few discussions, they're what we came up with," replied Sam.

"Unfortunately," said Brian. "That occurred before most of your current people were here. Have you done much to connect those values to your vision?"

"No."

"Over the six years, have there been times your people haven't lived those values?" asked Brian.

Sam sat silently.

"Then don't be surprised when your people don't stand for values you don't stand for. Culture doesn't come from posting values on a wall. It's a result of your Beings living those Beliefs. Your culture's the personification of your values."

"Wow," said Sam. "I could update the vision and values of Stamina. I need to match my vision with the current capabilities of the company, but I like our values. Are they wrong?"

"Just like a culture isn't good or bad, no value is right or wrong. But values only have value when people stand for them. Selecting values because they sound nice can create problems for a culture."

"Got an example?"

"Sure," replied Brian. "Let's use your core value, honesty. Tell me, are you an *honest* person?"

"Of course!"

"Okay, I believe you," said Brian. "Then tell me, when was the last time that you didn't tell the truth – even if it was a 'little white lie'?"

"It was yesterday," Sam slumped. "I told my wife I was too busy to clean the yard when I wasn't."

"Thanks for your honesty. Do you still think you're honest? Or are you honest until it's time to lie and return to honesty when you like?"

"I . . . I . . ." stammered Sam.

"I know that stings, but here's the lesson. You're either honest or dishonest. *You can't be both*. And that's where your values help . . . if you value them. Make sense?"

"Complete sense," answered Sam. "As CEO I have to live the values more than anyone else, huh?"

"Yup. Or why would anyone else?"

Brian and Sam continued their meeting until noon. During the three hours, Brian learned more about Stamina and helped Sam map out the company's vision. Brian also taught Sam about values by doing what a good consultant does: asking good questions.

At noon, Sam and Brian went to the cantina. Sam had lunch delivered for the staff. Since lunch was until 1 p.m., Brian spent the time meeting people. While Brian broke bread, Rajat approached Sam.

"Consultant?" Rajat said. "That's a good one, Sam. I was expecting another boring speech. I can't believe you got Coach Knight. How'd you do it?"

"Coach Knight?" asked Sam.

"Stop kidding," laughed Rajat. "Everyone knows him. . . . Come on, I know you avoid sports, but really? This guy wasn't just a coach, he's one of the university's best ever!"

Sam walked over to Brian, who was setting up the whiteboard for his presentation.

"You were a football coach?" asked Sam.

"Yes."

"Why didn't you mention it?"

"You never asked." Brian smiled. "Don't hold it against me . . ."

Brian's coaching history had Sam so distracted, he almost forgot Brian's introduction. When Sam finished, the group gave Brian a respectful ovation.

Brian explained he was a former football coach. Yes, he'd made big money and won big games, but his wife's cancer diagnosis shifted his priorities from football to family. He explained that even though he had left coaching, he'd always be a coach and his greatest skill was creating great cultures.

Brian mentioned he had learned a lot consulting for businesses and said he hoped what he'd learned would help Stamina reach its potential. His openness and vulnerability connected him the Stamina staff.

After his intro, Brian walked to the whiteboard and drew a small circle surrounded by three larger ones.

"I'm not a great artist, but what did I draw?" Brian said pointing to the circles.

"A bullseye!" said one of the engineers. "Is it a donut?" asked one member of the sales team. "Could be a truck tire!" shouted another woman over other answers from the staff.

Brian motioned for them to quiet down.

"What I drew was . . . your *attention*! There are a couple lessons from that exercise. First, before you're attentive to something, you must be made aware it exists. This week I'll make you more aware of the culture at Stamina and your role in it. Second, people can have different interpretations of the same thing until it's explained. My goal's not to make you guess at the culture here; I want everyone crystal clear. Does that make sense?"

Many of the staff nodded.

"After I share a story, you'll return to your work at Stamina. Throughout this afternoon, Wednesday, and Friday, I'll perform my checkup. I'll be assessing the health of the culture. And how I'll measure that 'health' is how your doctor measures your health: with information. My goal is to meet each of you and ask you questions. Why I'm telling you this is because I'll need honest answers, and I don't want you acting differently than normal. Do I have your commitment to be honest and authentic this week?"

This got some yesses from the group.

"Great!" said Brian. "Now a story to remind you what fuels a powerful culture. One day at work, a man got the call you see in movies . . . his wife was in full-blown labor! He raced for the hospital, but because he was staring at his phone's GPS, he narrowly missed a stopped car and crashed into a ditch. He was okay, but his car was stuck. A farmer who lived there came to help, and when the man explained his wife's situation, the farmer said, 'Don't worry. I got Old Thunder around back and he'll pull your car out.' The man felt a spark of hope - until he saw the horse. 'I'm sorry,' said the man, 'I don't know horses, but this one doesn't look healthy.' 'You're right.' said the farmer 'This horse's blind and can barely hear, but I know a trick that'll get your car out.' When the farmer tied Old Thunder to the car, the man gave up every expectation. But the farmer did something unexpected. The farmer yelled into Old Thunder's ear, 'Go Bessie, go Tank, go Racer, go Onyx, and you too, Thunder, let's goooo!' Hearing the farmer, Thunder pulled with the power of 100 horses! The car exited the ditch. Before the man sped off, he said, 'I don't believe what I saw. How'd you get him to do that?' The farmer replied, 'I learned that trick long ago. If Thunder thinks he's the only one pulling, he *won't do anything*. But that horse always works his hardest when he thinks he's on a *cool team*.'"

The staff got the message. Brian got another ovation.

7

A Little Push

"Knock, knock," sang Brian.

"Hey, Coach, is it 7 a.m.? There never seems to be enough time."

"It'll get better, Marcus," answered Brian as he scanned the office. "You're laying the foundation for everything. That's the longest part."

"So . . . what does my interior decorator think of the place?"

"I like what you've done with the Marcus Chase Memorial. Few recruits will come in here and not become part of this program. Where'd you get this older stuff? The 1944 program and old ticket stubs are cool."

"I know, right?" said Marcus. "I went 'all in' and made this place an extension of our locker room. I asked the admin team for some historical items. When I checked out what they had, it was hard to pick from all the great stuff."

"I like it. Makes me want to play here. You got a spot for a slightly over-the-hill linebacker?"

"Slightly?" Marcus coughed. "Let's stick to coaching me, coach. And as for 'all in,' I'm pleased to announce I got Gunny Gunderson as my head strength coach! He was excited and didn't deliberate. This place's hard to pass up."

"Perfect," Brian replied. "He'll be an asset. How's everything else going?"

"I have a few more staff interviews with previous coaches. I let the athletic director know I'm keeping a number of them. My relationship with the administration's been great, and they're supportive. My biggest challenge is salvaging a recruiting class. With signing day on February 1, I need to pull off a miracle."

"Sounds like you'll be pulling off a lot of plane flights too," said Brian. "I don't miss that part of the job. Recruiting is the future of your program. It's like shaving. If you don't do it every day you'll look like a bum. And recruiting's more than talented players; it's also about finding ones who match *who you want to be*."

"Who I want to be?"

"Sure," said Brian. "There are different styles a head coach can use to run a program. During your history, you've experienced a number of them. So . . . who will you be? The figurehead who shows around star recruits and famous alumni? Or will you have strong connections with your players or leave that to their position coaches? You could be the 'hands-off' coach in the golf cart or the 'hands-on' coach who's in on every drill. Coaches have had success with every style, so it's your choice."

"I hear that," answered Marcus. "And I've thought about it. I have more responsibilities now, so I'll need to let people do their jobs. But I never want to be that coach who doesn't know his players' names. A few players said they never got to know the last coach. To win right away, I have to remove that resentment, and be *available* for this team. I want them seeing me working harder than anyone."

"That's why I'm here."

"To show me I don't know what I don't know?" asked Marcus.

"And to encourage you to move forward when you do. Kinda like swimming with alligators . . ."

"Swimming with alligators?" repeated Marcus. "Where you going with that?"

"I'm going to Texas," smiled Brian. "There was a Texas oil tycoon worth hundreds of millions. Because his daughter had so many suitors, he worried they were only interested in inheriting his fortune. One day, he announced a competition in which one man would be chosen worthy of courting his daughter. He told all suitors to meet at his estate on the upcoming Saturday. That day, 25 men showed up. The tycoon showed them his amazing estate. On the tour, they stopped at the Olympic-sized pool. The suitors noticed it wasn't just filled with water, it was filled with alligators too! The tycoon started the competition. He had the suitors line up on one side of the pool and said whoever dove in and swam to the other side first could court his daughter. As the tycoon had planned, no one moved. The suitors kept wondering if anyone would jump in. Feeling satisfied no one was really interested in his daughter, the tycoon started walking back to his mansion. But then he heard a loud splash. The tycoon saw someone had jumped in! To the amazement of everyone, this man swam so fast the gators couldn't catch him. He reached the other side and exploded from the water. The tycoon was disappointed, but also impressed by the man's courage. He approached him and said, 'That's the most courageous thing I've ever seen! A man like you is worthy of courting my daughter and perhaps of inheriting my fortune. Someday you could have it all – the oil, the mansion, and the money. Now that you have won the competition, what do you want first?' 'What do I want first!?' the young man exclaimed. 'I want the name of the guy who *pushed me in!*'"

Marcus laughed out loud. "You never cease to amaze me. You've got a story for everything."

"Stories, Marcus, are a great way to teach. That one was to teach you I'll always be the coach who gives you a push when you need it."

Marcus smiled.

"Here's one," began Brian, "the office is looking better, but I noticed something missing from the brick. You cooking up any new ham?"

"Working on it, Coach. Those questions have helped, but it's hard. Trust me, I'm on it. I've come up with ideas about the environment I want to create. Want to hear those?"

"Of course."

"Okay," said Marcus. "I want an environment where the players work together, and not only feel welcomed and safe, but also valued and significant. I want a vibe where everyone feels respected and appreciated for their pursuit of excellence on and off the field."

"Nice. You're moving in the right direction. Defining the environment you want will lead to the culture you create. You just listed the *preconditions* for the culture you want."

"Preconditions?" asked Marcus.

"Yes, just like it's a precondition you carry the football to score a touchdown, you'll need environmental preconditions to score the culture you want. And once your culture's in place, your job gets easier – then you either coach *up* or coach *out*. Many coaches skip setting the preconditions. Then instead of enjoying the hallmarks of good team culture, they experience the *lagging indicators* of a bad one."

"Lagging indicators?" asked Marcus.

"A lagging indicator's something you see now because of something that's been happening for a long time. Just like you can't build a great culture overnight, a bad one doesn't just appear either. The lagging indicators of either good or bad cultures are the culmination of what's been adding up over time. For instance, lagging indicators of a good culture are *Positive Morale*, *Pride*, *Teamwork*, *Integrity*, and *Loyalty*. A great team may have them now, but they took time to develop. Bad cultures have lagging indicators, like *Poor Morale*, *Negativity*, *Mediocrity*, *Turnover*, and *Apathy*. If you understand that both cultures take time to develop, you'll see that you have influence over things that create the culture you want."

"I've been part of good and bad cultures," said Marcus. "Got any tips how to avoid the bad lagging indicators?"

"Sure. Constantly instill the preconditions you listed, and watch out for *culture killers*."

"Culture killers?"

"Yes," said Brian. "As a young coach, I wasn't good at spotting them. In fact, I contributed to them! But as my coaching improved, I spotted these killers and addressed them before they became bad lagging indicators."

"What are the culture killers?" asked Marcus.

"Some are harder to spot, and some are easy. But more important than spotting them is addressing them when you do. For instance, one killer is *gossip*. You know, players or staff getting together and talking negative about someone who isn't there! That gossip leads to another killer, *cliques*. The T in team stands for 'together.' When the team breaks into factions, a bad culture isn't lagging far behind."

"I've been on teams when cliques formed between the offense and defense and with certain positions too."

"That's why," said Brian, "you must address these killers and stop them before they stop your culture. Beside gossip and cliques, another killer's *ambiguity*. When players are unsure about the team's values or their role on the team, it's hard to buy into that team. So coaches who never make them clear take a clear path to bad culture."

"I've been on those teams too," said Marcus.

"But of all the culture killers, one leads to the worst problems."

"Which one's that?"

"That killer's *neglect*," said Brian. "When players are ignored or feel alone, rarely does anything positive happen. Neglect's a multiplier of other killers too. For instance, neglect can increase ambiguity, which creates insecurity or fear in a player. And when that player starts worrying about himself more than the team, that's when neglect leads to the biggest killer of all, *ego*."

"Ego?" repeated Marcus. "Yeah, being around alpha males, I know that one."

"The best teams I ever coached were filled with selfless players. I'm not saying they weren't concerned about themselves or their stats, but the needs of the team came first. When a player's all ego; that player gets selfish. And that's the opposite of team. The most selfless team I coached was your senior year. Yes, there were star individuals, but everyone did their best for the team first. By lowering ego and serving each other, everyone rose to a higher level."

"I agree, Coach," said Marcus. "I think about that team a lot. Especially Charlie."

"Yeah . . . I think about your linebacker group a lot. Who could forget the 'Three Musketeers?'"

"All for one and one for all," Marcus responded. "That was my favorite team. We loved playing and there wasn't ego. Man, I often think how things could be different now."

"You can't change the past," sighed Brian. "But you can change the future . . . especially of this program. And that change will rely on what you write on that brick. I suggest instead of letting your senior year remind you of bad things, why not take that team's biggest lessons and use them to make the culture here great."

"Lemons into lemonade, huh?"

"Yup," smiled Brian. "Every setback's a setup for a comeback."

"Seeing your comeback, Coach," said Marcus, "I'm glad you're back in the saddle. Enough about me – what had you so busy yesterday you couldn't help your favorite athlete?"

Brian told Marcus about his work with Stamina. Always being a connector, Brian had an idea that felt right.

"Listen, Marcus, for helping you, and because I'm drinking your seltzers, I want you to do something for me."

"Besides a motto for my brick?" joked Marcus.

"You mean my brick, kid," smiled Brian. "That's on loan. I know you're busy being an ESPN star, but I want you to meet with the guy Sam I spoke about. I have a feeling you have something to offer each other."

"Ugh, I'm busy, Coach. So many people compete for my time, I don't know."

"I understand, Marcus, but hear me out. Since I'm teaching you both about culture, at worst you compare notes and learn something. At best, you find synergies and help each other even more. Don't forget as a head coach, your network's one of your most valuable assets. All I'm asking for is one meeting."

"My office is looking better, though, don't you think?" smirked Marcus.

"Yes. As always, your coach is proud of you. . . . So will you meet this guy?"

"Do you ever get tired of being that Texas tycoon, Coach?" asked Marcus.

"Never. I'm always ready to give you another push."

8

Flea Circus

"Morning," Brian smiled as he exited his car. "You beat me here again, huh?"

Sam said, "I learned if you're on time, you're already late for something."

"Jeez! Already stealing my lines."

The two men walked into Stamina and took their positions in Sam's office. Sam pulled out his golden notebook.

"I gotta tell you, the team enjoyed Monday's talk, and meeting you too. I've continued examining the 'white spaces,' and instead of hiding from me, people actually said hello."

"Don't get too excited, kid," Brian grinned. "Even though they've made a small change, I've found some big changes that must happen to right this ship. When I asked for their honesty, they gave it!"

"Ugh. So what are your discoveries about Stamina?"

"This," Brian began, "is a consultant's toughest job – knowing the fine line between a 'want' and a 'need.'"

"What's that?" asked Sam.

"Well . . . in the past, some businesses brought me in to keep up with the Joneses. They never wanted to make real changes. Because I understood, I spent more time telling them what they wanted to hear than what they needed to hear. Hearing what you want is less painful than hearing what you need."

"I understand," said Sam. "I'm looking for needs. We have millions of people's money riding on Stamina, so know I can take it. Don't sugarcoat it . . . just be gentle."

"Okay," replied Brian. "Glad to hear because the only way you'll change the culture is by understanding where it is right now. Don't take it personally, but know some of what I will say stems from who you've shown your people you are as a person."

"I'm ready. . . ."

"Good," Brian said. "Although your Beings are nice people and talented enough to perform their jobs, the culture is holding Stamina back from performing at its best. From a 30,000-foot view, you have a culture of individuals. As you noticed, staff hide in their personal spaces throughout the building. This seclusion not only disconnects everyone, but it also slows everything down. You have the workspace set up for interaction, but the culture doesn't support it."

"I agree," nodded Sam.

"But I didn't just watch people," continued Brian. "I also did what a leader should do – sit with them individually, ask questions, and listen. That's where I discovered your staff likes what Stamina does, but they don't know the people they work with. I found backstabbing between your divisions, and the perception that each individual group is doing all the work. Did you know the engineers call themselves the 'A-team?'"

"No," chuckled Sam, "I hadn't heard that."

"Not a laughing matter, Sam. And neither's another thing I found . . . no one knows what *you* do here. They know you founded the company and you're in the building, but they don't know your role. They know you stay late, so they do the same in fear. And because they don't know where they stand with you, there's more stress, anxiety, and jockeying."

"You didn't sugarcoat that one."

"Welcome to the difference between a want and a need, kid," answered Brian. "There were positive things. I particularly enjoyed meeting the engineers. Although they see themselves as a separate entity, they have solid chemistry and enjoy their work. Stamina's not using its talent wisely. That's why you must raise your expectation of this flea circus!"

"Flea circus?"

"Yup," smiled Brian. "There's a funny thing about fleas you should know."

"Does this have to do with Vultures?" asked Sam.

"Not really, but this idea will produce less of them. Did you know fleas can jump over 60 times their body length?"

"Well," answered Sam, "I've heard they jump on animals."

"Yes, but think how amazing that is in relation to humans. If you were a 6-foot person who could jump 60 times that, that would be a jump of 360 feet! It'd be like leaping a tall building in a single bound!"

"Sounds super," quipped Sam.

"It is super and it relates to a super-leadership concept. You've heard of a flea circus, right?"

"Yes," said Sam, "weren't they fake?"

"Not at all!" exclaimed Brian. "In the 1800s and early 1900s, flea circuses were popular. Jewelers crafted miniature objects like chariots for fleas to pull. Because of a flea's powerful hind legs, the creativity of the craftsmen allowed simple fleas to perform complex shows for big crowds."

"Sounds interesting. What's this got to do with Stamina?"

"Everything," smiled Brian. "A flea circus training method can help the culture here. Flea circus owners were often asked how the fleas trained for tricks. Since people knew they jumped, they wondered why fleas didn't jump from the circus. Here's the answer. Yes, when a flea is placed in a lidless cage, it will jump out. But if a glass lid is placed over the cage, the fleas jump into the lid repeatedly until they learn to stop hitting the lid. Since the fleas then jump lower, the lid can be removed and they never jump out!"

"So what's that got to do with leadership?"

"Everything!" exclaimed Brian. "It's one of my big leadership lessons, even though it involves small insects. As the leader, you're responsible for the lid height at Stamina. The lid represents your expectations for the culture – your values, your rules, and how people should interact. Here's a big idea: the Beings at Stamina will rise or fall to the level of expectations you set for them. So raise that lid height and your Beings will rise to bigger challenges. But if you set the lid low, your culture will reflect the lowest level of Beliefs you tolerate."

"You've done it again," quipped Sam, taking notes.

"Thanks," replied Brian. "Now that you better understand your leadership role, I'll cover the final B of culture. That B concerns the reflection I just talked about."

"Reflection?"

"Yes," replied Brian. "Your culture will be a reflection of the lowest level of Beliefs you've instilled. The level of Beliefs has to do with lid height, but how that's reflected by your Beings is through their *Behaviors*. So, the third B of Culture is Behaviors. They're the *'how we do it.'*"

Sam wrote it down.

"Now you know the three Bs," began Brian. "Your Beings are your people, your Beliefs are the vision and values you give them, and their Behaviors are the ways they carry out your vision according to the values. All three Bs fit together in an order. They're also always in flux, and your job's to perform periodic checkups to assess them."

"Culture's getting clearer," said Sam.

"That's my job," smiled Brian. "To take something complex and make it simple, not the other way around. I have another idea you might like. I learned Stamina was founded on the programs you created. Because you identify as more programmer than CEO, we can use that to lead your culture."

"Really? What's the idea?"

"Don't think of yourself as the CEO for your culture . . ." began Brian. "Instead imagine you're the programmer coding in the Beliefs here. Just like the lid idea, if you properly program your Beliefs into your Beings, you'll get the Behaviors you want those Beings to run."

"Whoa!" laughed Sam. "I do like it! So, Beings are my hardware and Beliefs are the software. And the Behaviors indicate how the program runs. And . . . if the Behaviors aren't what I want, just like fixing bugs in a program, I change the code!"

"Couldn't have said it better myself! When you're examining the 'white space' at Stamina, you're looking at the Behaviors of your Beings. Those Behaviors are the ways people act and interact with each other and anyone else involved with Stamina. I call them *Cultural Exchanges*."

Sam wrote down both words.

"So backstabbing and hiding out aren't the Cultural Exchanges I want?" asked Sam.

"Nope," affirmed Brian. "But if you're seeing Behaviors you don't want, now you know to change the programming that caused them."

"It's a great idea."

"Thanks," continued Brian. "Here's one last idea about Behaviors before we go to lunch."

Brian grabbed his phone and handed it to Sam and said, "Watch this, and be ready – it's intense."

The video was of a rugby team. Sam wasn't familiar with rugby, but the clip was captivating. Sam watched as the team members screamed and danced together using powerful movements. With their tongues flashing and hands slapping, they chanted in an ancient language. As the intensity of the movements grew, Sam felt goosebumps. When the video ended, he asked, "What was that?"

"That, Sam, was the famous Haka of the New Zealand All Blacks. To some, the Haka might look like a choreographed dance to intimidate opponents, but there's more to it. This Behavior is the team's reflection and celebration of the Beliefs of their Maori culture. It's a ritual they perform before matches to honor the history of their country and their commitment to uphold that legacy. What they're actually screaming is less a 'war cry' as it's a reminder of their values."

"It was intense," said Sam.

"Yes," Brian answered. "And an example how Behaviors create *rituals*. Rituals are the most influential Behaviors your team can perform to uphold your culture. That was rugby, but if you've been around sports, many teams have rituals. And they don't have to be as complex or long as the Haka. They could be the way everyone says hello."

"I guess we don't have any rituals here?"

"Oh . . . don't be too sure. You have rituals about getting here early and hiding out. You have another about only approaching people when there's a problem. Cultures will develop rituals whether you consciously design them or not. So, as we change the culture at Stamina, new rituals will emerge."

"I hope so . . ." sighed Sam.

"I know so. Listen to your culture coach."

Sam and Brian went to the cantina. For lunch, Sam followed Rajat's recommendation and ordered Indian cuisine. Everyone enjoyed the meal and Rajat obviously enjoyed explaining the differences between the curries. After lunch, the staff returned to their chairs to listen to Brian.

"Hello again. After my talk, I look forward to meeting with more of you. Just remember to stay open and honest when I do. The information you've given me is helpful. Now I'm going to ask you for some more. So . . ." Brian continued as he moved to the white board, "someone tell me the groups of people involved with Stamina."

Rajat shouted out, "The engineers!" to which another engineer called out, "A-team!"

"Yes! I've heard about you guys." Brian wrote down "Engineers" on the white board and said, "Gotta have programs to sell, right?"

"Don't forget customer service," Dana said.

"Of course!" Brian wrote that down. "Once there's a program, people have to know how to use it. Anyone else?"

"Sales team!" shouted Brandon as he got a "whoop-whoop" from a few sales team members next to him.

"Yes!" said Brian. "Nobody can use a program they didn't buy, right?"

"Who else are we forgetting? Come on . . ." Brian prodded.

Lee called out, "Marketing!"

"Nice, Lee," said Brian, impressing both the group and Lee by remembering his name. "Can't sell anything if no one knows about it, right?"

"Anyone else . . .?" asked Brian, pointing at Sam.

"Sam!" some staff shouted.

"Glad you didn't forget your CEO," said Brian as he wrote those three letters. "Gotta have someone steer the ship! Anyone else? Come on. Who else's involved with Stamina?"

"Investors?" offered Dana.

"Good job, Dana," said Brian. "And let me help . . . in addition to investors who helped pay for this building and your equipment right down to this cantina, there's also the board of directors who Sam reports to."

"Anyone else?" Brian repeated, to no answer.

"There are still two groups of people you're leaving out and that says something about your culture. One of those groups is more important than any listed so far. The first group's your *vendors*. These people do many things at Stamina, from the lawyers who draft the contracts you use, to the CPAs who account for the money you make. Your vendors also print your marketing and clean up after you leave. Since they are also your teammates here at Stamina, someone tell me . . . has anyone seen the cleaners at Stamina?"

Multiple staff members raised their hands.

"Great. Anyone know their names?" Brian asked, and the hands lowered. "I hope you get the lesson. Everyone involved in Stamina does different things, but everyone counts. Imagine the garbage or toilets never got cleaned. Or no one reconciled money for payroll. Every role is important to what you do here. But the vendors were the first group you forgot to mention. The second group you forgot are the most important of all. . . . They're your *customers*!"

The group groaned.

"Yes," smiled Brian as he wrote the words. "You for-got them, didn't you? I'll teach you one number so you never forget them again." Brian flipped the page and wrote the number 12.

"On January 2, 1922," Brian began, "a big football game was happening in Texas. Texas A&M was playing Centre College, and the Aggies of A&M weren't the favorites. In fact, Centre College was the number-one ranked team in the country! Back then college teams didn't have 100 players like today. Sometimes all a team could muster was little more than the minimum of 11 players required to play. As the game wore on, the A&M coach realized his team might have a shot to win. He also realized his players were tiring. Because one of his players was helping reporters in the press box, the coach called him down. He told him to suit up and be ready to play if they needed him. As legend has it, when the game ended, that player was the lone A&M player left standing on the sidelines."

"Even though he never got into the game," Brian restarted, "standing on the sidelines ready to help became A&M's symbol of service. In every game since, the student body of A&M stands the entire game, ready to be the 12th man if they get called from the stands. If you follow football," Brian continued, "you might've heard of the 12th man. Today, crowds are often called the 12th man because they're so supportive of the team, it makes winning difficult for the opponents. Whether it's cheering so loud or distracting them, an interesting phenomenon is created: *home field advantage*. The idea of the 12th man goes beyond sports. It works in business too. Stamina needs its customers cheering so loudly that winning gets difficult for the competition."

Brian scanned the room.

"Without customers, there's no Stamina. Without customers to use your product, there's no reason to engineer, market, sell, or serve one. The 12th man is about loyalty, enthusiasm, and support. Your 12th man must be your biggest fan. To forget your customer is forgetting that 12th man – and if they feel forgotten, they can fire you whenever they want. Stamina cannot give up its home-field advantage."

Brian finished with a little bow. Before Brian left to meet with staff, Sam called him over.

"Another great talk," said Sam. "That last concept was powerful."

"You're welcome," replied Brian. "And hopefully that reminds you how valuable Dana's role is to Stamina. I suggest meeting with her and letting her know it. As for meetings, there's one more I'm requiring you to attend as part of your culture education."

"What meeting?" asked Sam.

"I'm also working on culture with the new head coach at the university," Brian said. "He was the man with me at the diner the night you and I met. Because you're both getting different lessons from me, I think comparing notes could help you learn faster. I spoke to him and he knows you'll be contacting him. I don't have a plan; I just want you to meet.

"I'll do it," said Sam, "and I'll be respectful of his time."

"Great, and here's some advice: when you meet him, instead of asking how he can help you, question how you can help him."

9

Home Cooking

Sam sat at the dinner table when Melissa returned late from another long day at work.

"Wow," said Melissa. "Caught you here twice in two weeks. You know, if you move that junk you could eat a meal there."

"Yeah, I don't know if I'd eat here, but I like getting work done."

Melissa pointed at Sam's golden notebook. "Still working with the guy from the diner? How's that going?" she said walking over to the fridge.

"Really well. This guy's opening my eyes to a lot of things I'm doing wrong. I haven't been a great leader at work . . . actually, I've been a lousy one."

"Well," said Melissa scanning the fridge for something edible, "that's what he's supposed to be doing, right?"

"Yeah," replied Sam, "but that's not the only reason I'm bummed. He's taught me I've been a lousy husband, too."

That got Melissa's attention. "Do you have something to tell me?"

"I'll start with, 'I'm sorry,'" answered Sam.

"Sorry for what?"

"Sorry for where our relationship's gone," answered Sam. "I mean, look at us. We're like two people passing for a few moments a day. We haven't spent much time together and with the holidays coming, it's my reminder we don't celebrate as a couple."

Melissa was stunned. Maybe it was the stress or fatigue from another long day, but she got aggressive.

"Look," she started, "don't blame this all on me. I have long hours, but you aren't Mr. Homemaker, either. Hell, this is the second time I'm talking to you in a week beside texts, and you're not good at those anymore!"

"What?" said Sam.

"I mean, come on, Sam. I know fundraising's no joke. But those last six weeks of pitch meetings flying all over the country were too much. First you'd call to say good night. Then that turned into texts, which turned into forgetting to text at all."

"I was wiped out!" answered Sam. "And I did that work for us. You think I wanna be a slave to investors? I'm trying to set up our future."

"Do I have to remind you," Melissa fired back, "that we're both working hard? Maybe this is perfect to tell you since I've been holding it in since last week. On Wednesday night in the conference room, the guys started joking about their wives and the stuff they complain about. I just remember sitting there feeling pissed. And not because they didn't notice I was the only woman there, but because I was doing their job *and* the work of their wives at home! There I am working and realize I'm the one who makes sure we have groceries, a clean house, clean clothes, and Christmas gifts! I don't know when it all became my job, but it did. I sat there resenting you and myself for letting it happen, and thinking if we keep going this way, there might not be a future to set up!"

Sam was shocked.

"Look Meliss, I started by saying I'm sorry. Sorry for the lack of communication. Sorry for the busy schedules and the missed texts."

"Well," said Melissa calming, "you should be sorry."

"And I am. I wanted you to know working with this consultant has opened my eyes about the business and us. He's challenging me about my vision and while sitting here writing, I realized I can't envision my future without you in it. I was complaining tonight because I want to spend more time with you."

"I feel the same way," said Melissa. "Maybe I got a little defensive there. The office is eating me up. As a woman around all the men at work, I hate the environment, and I'm questioning what it's all for. Being one of the only women in my practice, I feel I have to do twice as good a job to get noticed. I feel my mistakes are highlighted and blown out of proportion too. It's so much pressure, I'm not sure I want to keep this up."

"Being a lawyer?"

"I don't know . . . my whole life everyone told me to be a lawyer. That started my path from undergrad to law school to my law firm. Everyone was so proud, but along the way I forgot what I wanted. And now the path says I should make partner. After all the hard work to get here, I'm not enjoying it. The competitiveness is too much. I can't remember why I started, but I do know I wanted to make a difference . . . have some type of purpose . . . but where I am right now, I don't see that happening."

"What do you want to do?" asked Sam.

"I don't know entirely, but I always thought I was going to change how people viewed lawyers . . . do good and use my talents to help people. But look what happened – I'm trapped in a cutthroat job, expected to respond to emails at 2 a.m., and have zero control. Then they increased my billable hour requirements. Work rules my life . . . and I feel trapped."

"Trapped? Why not work somewhere else?" asked Sam.

"After all these years? I'm getting closer to partner. And each year I've gotten good raises. I know partnership is years away, but it's the carrot that's kept me going.

I even think that's a ploy because the likelihood of making partner is zero."

"Zero? Why say that? You're great at what you do."

"It's not about being great," said Melissa. "It's about fitting the 'mold.' I started with 60 people in my class and only two of them are counsel and none have made partner. There are so few female partners, I guess it's something I wanted to prove to myself and the world. But law firms are geared toward men. There's real discrimination and that pushes qualified women out because they don't want to deal with it."

"I just heard you hate your job. Why partner with that? And as for money, we're doing great. We aren't hurting here, you know. And what's money when we're too busy to enjoy it anyway?"

Melissa thought before she answered. "I've been on this track so long, I haven't taken the time to question why. Maybe I wanted the lawyer title or prestige of partner, but that's not what I'm about anymore. The rush of the city's over and I'm worn out. I know my mom would be disappointed, but . . . what about you? Would you be okay if I did something else?"

"Of course! I'd support whatever you wanted to do. The best advice I have is to ask yourself, 'What's the worst thing that could happen?' If the answer's that you try something new and it doesn't work out, just go back to the shark tank you're in right now!"

"You're right," said Melissa. "I never thought like that. What about you?"

"What about what?"

"Do you want to do something besides Stamina? We're kinda in the same boat. Our jobs have us doing things we don't enjoy."

"Actually," began Sam, "the last couple weeks have reminded me how Stamina started and *why* it started. I don't dislike work. Don't get me wrong, there are parts of my job that I don't like, but I still like creating programs and I'm proud of Stamina. I just need to improve as a leader and fix some things. But why I waited up to talk to you wasn't to argue; it was because I want to fix things with you, too."

"You should know better than to argue with a lawyer," smiled Melissa. "About that shark tank, I've got a lawyer joke you might like."

"You know I can't resist those," replied Sam.

"Okay, then answer this," started Melissa. "What's 1000 lawyers on a sinking ship?"

"What?"

Melissa smiled and said, "A good start."

"Good one, babe. And you just reminded me of another idea I wanted to cover. . . ."

10

From Me to We

"I can't believe it's Friday," said Sam.

"Time flies . . ." Brian joked.

". . . when you're having fun," agreed Sam. "I've done so much working *in* this business I forgot the enjoyment from working *on* it."

"Watch it, kid. Working on your culture isn't a sometimes thing, it's an all-the-time thing. Imagine Stamina's a child. You don't nurture a child occasionally, right?"

"No," nodded Sam.

"That's right," continued Brian. "A child, just like your culture, requires constant nurturing."

"Even though I don't have kids, I understand. In fact, I often call Stamina my 'baby.' I hope I become a better parent than the leader I've been."

"Don't beat yourself up," smiled Brian. "There's an interesting thing about life. The older you get, the more you'll realize you were never taught the important stuff. For example, I was taught nothing about being a husband. Or about women! And when I got home from the hospital with my first child, I was clueless. Even when I knew about football, I didn't know about coaching people. Life's an exam, and unfortunately you often get the answers after the test."

"That's true. I knew about programming, but when I started Stamina, I quickly learned I needed sales, marketing, and communication skills because I didn't have them."

"Yeah," chuckled Brian, "would be easier if your business or marriage came with an instruction manual, right?"

"I wish."

"Well, in both cases, you discovered a need for knowledge and you're seeking it out. Growth's about awareness. Now you're aware of the importance of culture and working on that too."

"And I'm writing the manual." Sam smiled, pointing to his notebook.

"Correct," said Brian. "Since today's the last day of the checkup, let's review to see what you've learned."

"I'm ready."

"Okay," began Brian, "tell me the three Bs of Culture."

"That's easy," answered Sam. "Beings, Beliefs, and Behaviors."

"Good. Now tell me the who, what, and how of the three Bs."

Sam answered, "Beings represent 'who we are,' Beliefs are 'what we stand for,' and Behaviors are 'how we do it.'"

"Right again! Those definitions are important. But now I'll make culture even easier and summarize the three Bs into one word. Actually, you'll do it. So . . . what's your one-word summary of culture?"

Sam didn't answer.

"Okay. I'll help you. Of those definitions of the three Bs, what's the one word they have in common?"

Sam thought and exclaimed, "We!"

"Bingo!" yelled Brian. "Culture's about that one word – *we*. Combining your Beings, Beliefs, and Behaviors produces a 'we.' How Stamina's 'we' looks, acts, and, therefore, feels like is based on your three Bs. Since the three Bs are under your leadership, you have a choice: create the 'we' you want, or accept the 'we' you get. And your 'we' won't only determine the economic success at Stamina; it'll also determine Stamina's long-term survival."

"Wow . . ." said Sam, "more pressure."

"No pressure, no diamonds, kid. And I'm not adding pressure, I'm removing it. Being aware of your leadership responsibilities can seem overwhelming. But that's better than feeling powerless and watching your business fail."

"I believe you," said Sam.

"Don't worry. Once you create your 'we,' and then give Stamina the 'big why,' everything gets easier."

"The big why?" Sam asked.

"Yes," said Brian, "the big why makes your three Bs work together. You ever heard, 'If you have a big enough why, you'll figure out how'?"

"Sure."

"Well, for your Beings to carry out your Beliefs with their Behaviors, they'll need a big enough 'why' to do it," said Brian. "And that 'big why' is your *mission.*"

Sam wrote in his notebook.

"As a consultant, I wasn't only working with businesses. I also consulted with professional sport teams, universities, and military organizations. Although I was teaching, I was learning too. I learned about missions at Fort Benning working with the Army Rangers."

"Whoa," said Sam. "The Rangers? Those guys are badass."

"Yes, they are," Brian reminisced. "During my weeks observing them, I studied their training, and got to try their obstacle course!"

"Sounds fun."

"Not exactly," answered Brian. "It was scary! Although the training and title of Ranger may seem glamorous, don't forget they've got a dangerous job . . . and they face that danger with a smile."

"Danger or not," nodded Sam, "everyone dreams about being one of those soldiers."

"Like they say," smiled Brian. "Everyone wants to be a Ranger until it's time to do Ranger stuff. I remember a higher-ranking soldier explaining the money invested into producing each Ranger. He asked me, 'Do you believe we invest millions into each of these soldiers?' I said yes, and then came the lesson. He said, 'But did you know they have no value?' When I didn't answer he smiled and finished his statement with '. . . until they have a mission.'"

"Sam, your staff have things in common with the Rangers. You've carefully selected them, equipped them with high-tech equipment, and trained them for their job. But that investment doesn't matter . . . until you give them a mission. You gave them the 'how' and 'what,' but to do them, they need a big 'why.' That 'why' is the mission. And unfortunately, you've kept your mission top secret."

"Yeah? How do I make it public?"

"Easy," answered Brian. "First, precisely define the mission, and then repeat it consistently until it influences everyone's behavior."

"When we created our values," said Sam, "we also worked on a mission statement. It's the sentence on our stationery: 'Powering the people who power businesses.' Is that what you mean?"

"Call your mission whatever you want, but only you can make the call if it's still relevant. Just like the Rangers, missions can and will change."

"Ugh," grunted Sam. "Does Stamina need a new mission?"

"I can't decide that," answered Brian. "I explain the importance of your mission, not what it should be. That's up to you. But your mission should inspire your Beings to be better versions of themselves. The greatest people in history didn't only have talent; they had a bigger 'why' than most people. And the closer a person feels their mission is to their purpose . . . that's where great-ness happens."

"I understand. We need some greatness around here again."

Brian smiled and said, "Then accept your mission to come up with your mission."

Until noon, Sam and Brian continued covering other key performance indicators like revenue and profit. Sam's anxiety increased when he realized Stamina's gross revenue had leveled off. Even though Stamina had grown in size and raised more capital, the company wasn't producing more money. At noon, they visited the cantina for the final staff lunch-and-learn.

"I've got good news and bad news," Brian began. "Which one first?"

The majority answered, "Bad news!"

"Man, it's always bad news first. Okay, the bad news . . . this is our last lunch together," Brian said pouting.

There were boos from the staff.

"Okay, okay. But the good news is, over the last week, I've given you some big ideas about teams. Today I'll teach you one word that separates good teams from great." Pointing to the whiteboard, Brian continued, "On Monday, I taught you that each of you will work harder when you're part of a cool team. On Wednesday, you were reminded who makes up your team at Stamina – most importantly, your customers. Today you'll learn the 'magic word' that connects you to this team."

Brian paused.

"Since you're a creative group, I need you to crea-tively imagine a scenario. Are you ready?"

There were yesses.

"Anyone have a favorite sports team?" Brian asked.

Rajat called out, "You know mine, Coach!"

"Nice," continued Brian. "Well, regardless of whether your favorite's the same as Raj's, picture yourself as your team's greatest fan. Imagine your favorite team made it to the world championship! And not easily. Imagine they've come from behind in every game, and reached the championship as huge underdogs. Got it?"

Everyone was engaged.

"Okay. Because you're the team's greatest fan, you aren't watching it on TV; you're at the game! So picture yourself there, dressed in the team's colors – your face is painted in them too. Now imagine your team's losing. And not by a little, but a lot. But instead of giving up, your team fights back, and with almost no time left, they do the improbable and win the game!"

Brian paused for a few cheers.

"Now imagine you flew home, and the next day you're here at work. Imagine I didn't hear what happened during the greatest experience of your life. For your final picture, imagine I ask you, with paint still on your face, 'Who won the game? . . . What would you say?'"

A few staff called out, "We won."

"What?" asked Brian. "As your team's greatest fan, is that how quietly you'd say it? No way! You'd be jumping and screaming, "We won! We won!" Brian said jumping to the group's laughter.

Brian composed himself and asked, "Why did you say 'We?' You know you didn't play in the game, right?"

"But we felt like we did!" answered Rajat.

"Precisely, Raj!" Brian said. "And that's the feeling we need at Stamina. The important word is *we*," said Brian writing a W and an E on the whiteboard. "My goal is to make Stamina your favorite team. Each of you is a player for this team, and everything you do matters. Just like with a sports team, when one player does something good, the other players benefit. So, like a touchdown on the field, you should celebrate a new program or sale. Those celebrations will transform your thinking from *me to we*. With that selfless mindset, when Stamina hits a major goal, you'll shout, 'We won!'"

After the meeting, Sam stopped Brian before he left to observe the staff.

"Another amazing day," said Sam. "Thanks again."

"Thank me by using this stuff," Brian countered. "And thank you for your confidence in me to present. I've enjoyed it and hope we continue to work together."

"Be sure of that! I've spoken with the board and they agreed to ongoing consulting. I'd pay for it myself if they didn't. You'll be glad to hear Coach Chase and I are meeting next week too."

"Great about both of those," smiled Brian. "Like you, Coach Chase needs help with his mission. About the ongoing work, don't you want my checkup diagnosis before you decide to keep me around?"

"Nope, I'm convinced I have the culture coach for the job."

11

Latin Lesson

Following Brian's last-minute instructions, Sam entered Marcus's office without any expectations, but he did bring two egg-and-cheese biscuits and coffees.

"Hi, I'm Marcus Chase." Marcus extended his hand. "You must be Sam. Coach Knight told me a lot about you."

"Nice to meet you, Coach. I hope what he said was positive. He said good things about you . . . like you're his greatest student."

"Sweet," laughed Marcus. "Could be . . . Coach has been teaching me for a long time. He's got a lesson wrapped in a story for every occasion."

"I know what you mean," Sam said, raising the bag and coffees. "I wouldn't have brought these without his lesson on breaking bread."

"Hmmm, let's sit and test out that lesson."

As they sat, Sam looked around the room. "You a football fan?" asked Marcus.

"Not really. I played when I was little, but there was pressure on me to succeed. That pushed me away from sports. Since my dad was a computer guy, he got me interested in coding. I thank him for my company. What about you? Are you a fan of computers?"

"Umm, well . . . I use one," said Marcus, pointing to his computer.

Sam felt the conversation going dry.

"I appreciate your time today." Sam reached for small talk. "Brian said you're extremely busy . . . but he was persistent that we meet up – sorry if it's a hassle."

"Yeah, I'm busy but . . . to be honest," said Marcus. "I'm helping you because you're helping him."

"How?"

"By giving him something to do again," replied Marcus. "Ever since his wife's passing, he isn't the same guy.

He's cut people off, including me. But lately he's excited again. Excited about you and your business. You've given him the gift he needed. . . ."

"Gift?" repeated Sam. "He's done all the giving so far."

"Working with you reminded him who he is. And he still has something valuable to contribute. That's something everyone needs."

"I didn't realize," said Sam. "He's been helping me so much, I felt guilty not giving back."

"Letting him help you is giving back," said Marcus. "He's a coach, so he needs to help people."

"Don't worry. My life's such a mess, he'll be in the coaching business for a while."

"Now," laughed Marcus. "There's something we have in common."

"Brian also mentioned we're both fixing our team culture. He's given me a lot of assignments, and said to compare them with yours. Need any help?"

"This brick's been my toughest assignment," answered Marcus

"You got a gold brick? Lucky you. I got this gold notebook."

"Ha!" smiled Marcus. "Then you *are* someone he likes. I've gotten a few of those too. He wasn't kidding about how valuable they'd be."

"Yeah," agreed Sam. "He's challenged me to write some tough things down."

"Try writing them on a brick," said Marcus. "My assignment's to come up with my motto for this season. Coach wants me to decide what my culture stands for, and sum it up with a slogan. He wants that slogan on this brick."

"Like a mission statement? Brian taught me his three Bs and I'm working on my mission to guide my 'we.'"

"Ahh, the three Bs, huh?" smirked Marcus. "Yeah, a motto's similar to a mission. The motto anchors the team to the culture while carrying out the mission. It's a quick reminder what your culture stands for. So, using Coach's three Bs, a motto's a couple words that summarize the Beliefs to guide the Behaviors. As I've seen, if your motto's strong enough, your 'we' gets stronger."

Sam wrote it down and asked, "So what've you come up with? Maybe I could help."

"I've wracked my brain. I keep coming back to old mottos from previous teams, but Coach wants something original. I have one idea, but it doesn't feel right."

"What is it?" asked Sam. "I'm not a sports guy, but I have created solid names for programs at Stamina. I use a simple process – I ask you questions, you start talking, and perhaps we find the answer together. So . . . what've you been thinking?"

"Okay," replied Marcus. "Because I want the team to connect with my philosophy, I thought about an important but tragic time in my life. Before I was a coach, I had a nice career in the NFL. Instead of being famous for my midgame tackles, I was best known for my pregame ritual."

"What was that?"

"Before every game, I'd fire myself up. Because of my intensity on the sidelines, the cameras caught it on film and I've been known for it ever since."

"So is high energy something you want in your culture?" asked Sam.

"Yes, but my idea's about why I acted that way. I didn't get amped up to intimidate my opponents . . . it was something deeper."

"Okay . . ." led Sam. "What was that?"

"Right before my pro career started, I lost my best friend. It was horrible. My dream of playing in the pros was happening, but I felt guilty. Life felt so unfair, I thought about giving up. But I got a wake-up call, and realized not playing was the worst way to honor my friend. So instead of his death bringing me down, it brought me up. His passing reminded me that life's short. I'd taken things for granted and wouldn't do it again. When I realized football wasn't forever, I never took a play off again. I began playing every down like it was my last. That mindset spilled into everything I did. I took each meal and workout more seriously. The more I demanded my best in the present moment, the more successful I became on and off the field."

"Thanks for sharing that," said Sam. "If I understand, your idea's about focusing and taking nothing for granted. Any ideas for a motto around that?"

"I used to call my philosophy 'every rep, every set.'"

"So . . ." said Sam, "what does that mean to you?"

"It means taking nothing for granted. Down to the littlest things – every thought in your head or every heartbeat. When my friend died, I realized I took the miracle of my heart beating for granted. Although you may get two billion heartbeats in your lifetime, when it's over, no amount of money can buy one beat back. When my friend passed, I knew his beats were gone, so I committed never to waste one again. You only get one heart, right?"

In a spark of inspiration, Sam typed something into his phone, smiled, and said, "I found something for your brick."

"What d'ya got?" said Marcus.

"Okay. When you were explaining 'Every rep, every set,' I liked it, but felt it needed the 'coolness factor.' Something cool that your players would like, like a secret code."

"Alright . . ." said Marcus.

"Then you said something that hit me. I get how not taking something for granted helps your players focus on every play, workout, and meal . . . but you went deeper. You got me with two words."

"And those were . . . ?" asked Marcus.

"Your philosophy isn't about big things – it starts with little things. When you brought your whole philosophy down to every heartbeat, you got me with *One heart*."

Sam checked Marcus's reaction.

"I wanted to add some 'coolness' by making this more like a code only the team would understand," continued Sam. "And on a hunch, that's when I found something for your brick. . . ."

"Give it to me."

"How about *Cor Unum*?" Sam asked. "That's Latin for 'one heart.' It sounds cool and summarizes your philosophy down to the smallest common denominator."

"Cor unum . . ." Marcus mumbled. "Cor unum . . ." he said louder. "I . . . love . . . it!" Marcus gave Sam a high five and told him, "You're really saving me. Why'd you go with Latin?"

"I studied Latin."

"Latin? Who does that anymore?" laughed Marcus.

"Computer nerds, I guess."

"How do you spell that?" asked Marcus.

"C-O-R and U-N-U-M," replied Sam.

"What's your shirt size?" asked Marcus.

Sam answered, "Medium," and Marcus produced a team T-shirt.

"Since you gave that to me, I'm giving this to you. For helping with the motto, welcome to the team."

"Glad to help," smiled Sam. "It was a pleasure building with you. With that motto out of the way, got any other problems I can help with?"

Marcus and Sam met for another 30 minutes, sharing their challenges and the lessons Brian had taught them. As Sam was leaving, Marcus said, "Today was great. I'm glad we got together."

"Me too," said Sam holding up his new shirt.

"But I did the talking today. We solved one of my problems, but not any of yours."

"Not true. I got some ideas and I'm helping you because I think you're helping your coach too." Sam winked.

Marcus smiled, slapped Sam's shoulder, and thought to himself, "Smart kid."

After Sam left, Marcus worked on his new motto. He took notes on what Cor Unum meant to him. By the end of the day, he was so confident about the words, Marcus used permanent ink to write them on his brick.

On his drive to Stamina, Sam was also energized. Brian's advice of breaking bread and seeking first to help had worked. Then Sam had his second big idea of the day. He called Rajat and yelled into the speaker, "Raj, you won't believe where I just was! I've got an idea you'll love . . . and a shirt too!"

12

The Diagnosis

"Great to have you back," said Sam. "You've brought positive energy to this place. I received positive feedback from the staff too."

"Happy to help," said Brian. "I've enjoyed meeting everyone. Now, as for feedback – the doctor is in . . . and I'm excited to share what I discovered during my checkup. I have a major finding for you too. Just remember, this diagnosis won't be as positive your staff's feedback about me, okay?"

"I'd love 'want to hears,' but I'm prepared for 'need to hears' too."

"Great attitude," said Brian. "Over my three days, I examined the culture. During that exam, I checked Stamina's 'Vitals of Culture.' I compiled everything to create my diagnosis, prognosis, and treatment plan for Stamina to turn things around."

"Give it to me straight, doc," joked Sam. "Can we save this place? I'm like an anxious patient looking for hope from my culture doctor."

"Ha! I'll stick with culture coach. Then I don't have to change my business cards. I wouldn't be helping you if there wasn't hope, kid," smiled Brian. "Hope's the last thing a coach should take away from anyone. Be assured there's hope for Stamina . . . the fact that you're driving a Zodiac gives me confidence."

"A Zodiac?"

"Not the horoscope kind," laughed Brian. "More like the Jacques Cousteau kind. A Zodiac's an inflatable boat known for speed and portability. You ever see one?"

"Yes," Sam replied. "They're fast right?"

"Yes, Because of their unique design, Zodiacs aren't only fast, but they can carry heavy loads too. If you've ever ridden in one, it's a comfortable ride."

"Can't say I have," answered Sam. "But what's a Zodiac boat got to do anything?"

"Being the leader of Stamina's like driving a Zodiac. Stamina doesn't have many people and is mobile and fast. So, as the driver, you can make quick decisions and implement them rapidly. Larger businesses don't allow rapid change to happen. I call them aircraft carriers."

"Alright," said Sam. "Is smaller an advantage?"

"For changing culture? Of course!" replied Brian. "Stamina can still stop on a dime and turn. An aircraft carrier takes forever to turn a few degrees. So, as you hear my diagnosis, don't get discouraged – imagine Stamina's a Zodiac ready to nimbly turn where it needs to go."

"That helps. I forget we're still a small business. So you think Stamina's going to make it?"

"Cutting to the chase again? As your 'culture doctor,' that reminds me of a joke. . . . A man came home crying from the doctor. His worried wife asked what was wrong. The husband replied, 'I can't say. It's awful.' As he continued crying, the wife asked again, 'What did the doctor say that has you so upset?' The man again replied, 'No, I can't tell you. It's awful.' Finally the wife grabbed him and said, 'Tell me! What did the doctor say?' The man calmed himself and said, 'The doctor said I need to take a pill every day for the rest of my life.' The wife was confused and said, 'That's not so bad, people take pills every day,' The man started crying again and said, 'No, you don't understand.' The wife tried to reassure him and said, 'It's perfectly normal to need a prescription every day for the rest of your life.' Because he kept crying, his wife began to panic and said, 'Enough! What don't I understand?' Then the man opened his hand and said, 'He only gave me *two pills*!'"

Brian smiled. "So, to reassure you, I'm prescribing *a lot* of pills."

"Whew," replied Sam. "Before I hear your diagnosis – do you think Stamina's worth saving?"

"Sam, leaders often ask me that question. Maybe it's losing touch with their business, but a leader often needs a fresh set of eyes to determine whether their business is still viable. After examining Stamina, it's not only worth saving, it's mandatory! And not because you raised millions in investment capital. Stamina provides a valuable service to so many companies! But don't get overconfident. Many businesses provide valuable services and go out of business. After going over your numbers, I see that Stamina's profitable and has the tools to generate more money. Your product's also cool and online learning like yours will continue to be in demand."

"I appreciate that," said Sam. "When is the bad news . . ."

"No time like the present," replied Brian. "Everything I mentioned was found from tests I administered. During my interviews I performed a 'trust fall' on your Beings, an 'eye exam' on your Beliefs, and an 'energy system test' to assess Behaviors. During my eye exam, I checked if your staff's vision matched Stamina's and how clearly they saw themselves fitting in here. Unfortunately, the vision at Stamina is blurry, at best."

Sam nodded.

"To assess Stamina's Behaviors, I challenged everyone's energy systems by checking their enthusiasm for their work and other staff members. I determined that spirit and energy levels are low and few people are interested in going the 'extra mile.'"

Sam took notes.

"Finally, my trust fall assessed the connections between your Beings. Not surprisingly, trust levels were also low."

"No, nothing surprising there," agreed Sam.

"There is something that may surprise you. Before I tell you, I've got another joke. A man went to see his doctor. The doctor asked, 'What's the problem?'" Brian pointed his index finger and said, "'Well doc, everything hurts. It hurts when I touch here and here and here,'" as Brian poked himself on his leg, stomach, and arm. "The doctor was confused and said, 'Does it hurt anywhere else?' The man replied, 'Yes! It hurts here and here and here too.'" This time Brian touched his foot, nose, and hip. "The doctor thought for a second and grabbed the man's finger. The man yelled, 'Ouch! What'd you do that for?' And the doctor replied, I just confirmed my diagnosis. You've got a broken finger!'"

Sam and Brian chuckled.

"Like that joke," Brian began, "Stamina has one problem causing all the rest. When we fix that, most of the pain'll go away. So here's my diagnosis. . . . You've got a classic case of *Vitamin L Deficiency*."

"Vitamin L?"

"Yes," replied Brian, "and the L stands for leadership. Every one of Stamina's problems – from blurry vision and lack of spirit to the absence of trust – stems from a leadership deficiency. Instead of a broken finger, Stamina has a broken leader."

"Ugh. But it's correct. I've been responsible for everything you mentioned."

"Go easy on yourself," Brian urged. "The diagnosis tells you the illnesses affecting the health of your business. But this diagnosis doesn't have to be permanent. The actions you take will affect the prognosis."

"What's the prognosis for a business with a broken leader?" asked Sam.

"Depends," replied Brian. "Many leaders never accept or admit they're the problem. When that happens, their company usually continues on with increased staff turnover and decreased profit. Then after a few years of cutting costs, those companies usually fail."

"Seems like we're moving in that direction."

"But you're driving a Zodiac," answered Brian. "Now that you know the problems, you can follow my treatment plan. If you take consistent action, Stamina's health will improve. Then my prognosis for Stamina becomes a long, healthy life."

"I accept the diagnosis and admit I can be a better leader. What's the treatment plan?"

"Not so fast," replied Brian. "That's a huge step to admit when you're wrong. Be proud of yourself for that. Before we cover the treatment plan, there's a major finding I discovered. It could be a big breakthrough for Stamina."

"What's that?"

"Okay," answered Brian. "Because I'm not technologically advanced, I didn't understand what Stamina did. Your staff kept mentioning sales and training. But as I examined your service, I realized you're pioneering something bigger. Stamina isn't a sales or training company that powers a business – Stamina is *the* company that changes how businesses communicate! Your product isn't training. You give businesses stamina by improving their communication!"

Sam sat back in his chair. After a deep breath, he said, "That *is* huge! This idea has endless possibilities for our software! We can communicate anything a business wants to teach. I have to think about this. . . ."

"Do you like the idea?"

"Like it? I *love* it!" said Sam. "That could change everything here. It's mind-boggling."

"Remember," Brian replied, "nothing happens overnight. It's an idea to work with and work on. I'll help with that. But before you go changing your business model, let's get back to changing your culture."

"Okay," said Sam as he wrote down notes. "Now, where were we?"

"Since culture's all about communication," started Brian, "I'll use that concept to explain my five-step treatment plan. Cultural problems result from a breakdown of communication, so each step's designed to build it up. Follow the plan and the levels of communication will improve."

"Got it."

"The first two steps involve things I've already prescribed," Brian began. "The first step's called *Language Lessons*. For a culture to communicate effectively, the Beings have to speak the same language. Right now, that's not happening at Stamina. As indicated from the eye exam, people say different things about the vision. Step 1 of this plan is to continue to create clarity about Stamina's vision, values, and mission. And to teach that language, you'll stick with Step 2 of the treatment plan."

Sam wrote notes.

"Step 2 involves a *Change in Diet* for your staff. I don't mean stocking the cantina differently. I'm talking about breaking bread with your staff. This'll help you build trust, but they'll also learn about you and your vision. I'd suggest these lunches take place consistently. You could book lunches or make your schedule available for staff to pick dates. Either way, the goal is consistent meals with your Beings."

Sam jotted notes as Brian continued.

"Once Stamina's language is in place, Step 3 is to increase the energy level at Stamina. Step 3 is *Group Therapy*. In Step 2, you're meeting individually. In Step 3, the object is to get everyone interacting outside of the office. Whether or not you call these social events, the point is to make Stamina more social. Get creative. You don't need ideas right now, but you must commit to regular staff events outside the workplace."

"I have some ideas," smiled Sam.

"Good," replied Brian. "After Group Therapy, Step 4 involves *Dressing for Success*. I noticed that no one wears any Stamina gear. I'm not saying you need a dress code, but the word 'uniform' can influence your culture."

Sam asked, "Uniform? We let people wear what they want."

"I know. But think about a sports team. A uniform involves distinctive clothes to identify people from the same organization. Those clothes lead to the power of affiliation by making people feel part of something bigger."

"When Marcus gave me a shirt the other day," nodded Sam, "I did feel more connected to the team."

"Boom! Marcus knows 'uniform' isn't just a noun. It's an adjective too. So when your Beings are 'uniform,' they're consistent in Beliefs and Behaviors. Their clothes and your logo can be powerful reminders of that. Your logo's cool and it isn't used enough. And your people need some gear. Something cool they'd be proud to wear. And it's good marketing too."

"Yeah, I love our logo," said Sam. "You're right . . . I don't even have any Stamina gear! How can I lead with pride if I'm not showing any to my people?"

"Get some people's advice on clothes," advised Brian. "Dana and Rajat could help. There's nothing worse than spending money on stuff people don't like."

"Agreed. I can do these. That leaves Step 5 . . ."

"Step 5 could be the most important one, Sam," Brian explained. "I call it '*Home Care*.' Leaders rarely understand that culture starts at home, not in the office. I learned that the hard way. I went through a tough time and wasn't getting support at home. But it wasn't my wife's fault; it was mine. Because I didn't involve her, she wasn't interested in my job. Being home only drained more of my energy. By worrying about work at home and home at work, my performance suffered at both."

"What did you do?"

"The most important thing," answered Brian. "I got her involved with my life. And my kids too. When they became part of my career, they supported me. And when they supported me, I became a better coach. No championship would've meant much without them by my side."

Sam sat silently.

"Today you asked if Stamina was worth saving," started Brian. "Let me ask you – is your marriage is worth saving?"

"Absolutely. I love my wife more than I love my business. I have a cultural problem there too. But I'm optimistic I can fix it."

"Culture's like marriage," smiled Brian. "It only works when you work on it. I'm no marriage expert, but I think I can help."

13

Alignment

"That's what I'm talking about!" exclaimed Brian, looking around Marcus's office. "Goodbye Marcus Chase Memorial!"

"Coach!" said Marcus. "This better be right. I don't have the nerve to ask to paint the walls three times!"

"You nailed it! I'm proud of you, and this is something to be proud of. I know I pushed you, but don't you feel inspired walking in here?"

"Yes," nodded Marcus. "You're right again."

Taking his usual seat, Brian asked, "How've things been?"

"Busy, but I feel good going into the break," replied Marcus. "I've selected my staff and recruiting trips are planned. I kept a few commits and feel good about some others. And Gunny's connecting with the players. They love his workouts."

"Great," smiled Brian.

"Here's Christmas gift number 1," said Marcus, pulling out a present.

"What's this?" Brian asked as he unwrapped the present. "Spam? You got me a can of Spam?"

"You said get rid of the old ham," replied Marcus.

"I guess I did. But I didn't say give it to me!"

"Ha . . . I don't need it anymore, Coach. Your assignment was tough, but the work was worth it. I have my motto and it's original," Marcus said as he handed the golden brick to Brian.

Brian read the words "Cor Unum."

"Cor Unum . . ." said Brian. "It means 'one heart,' right?"

Marcus looked disappointed. "Man . . . does everyone know Latin? First Sam and now you."

"Sam saw this?"

"No, Coach," replied Marcus, "Sam came up with it! Well, not with the idea, but he found the Latin phrase. Our meeting went well. He's a good kid."

"I'm glad that worked out," said Brian. "Now . . . tell me about this motto."

"I was explaining your assignment, and Sam got me talking. I told him about how Charlie's passing inspiring me to develop my 'Every rep, every set' philosophy. That idea symbolized not taking things for granted and doing everything to the best of your ability – even little things like plays on the field, meals at the table, and sleep in the bed. I broke it down further to every beat of your one heart. That's where Sam got the Latin phrase. So, Cor Unum represents taking nothing for granted because your time and ability are limited. I want players inspired to optimally develop their gifts."

"Nice work," said Brian. "I love that this motto's personal to you. The vulnerability you'll share about Charlie and its origin is powerful. And the words Cor Unum are unique. You took this from motto to *maxim*."

Marcus smiled.

"But . . . you still have to determine exactly what Cor Unum means."

"What?" asked Marcus.

"Don't take this the wrong way. The motto's good. But your explanation must be clearer. It needs to involve the team too. Take Cor Unum from 'me' to 'we.'"

"Doesn't it involve the team?" asked Marcus.

"Not from what I heard," said Brian. "Remember, 'every rep, every set' was your personal philosophy to for individual behavior. That's a lot of 'me.' But for Cor Unum to work, it must serve as a constant reminder how to behave as a 'we.'"

Marcus sighed and said, "I thought I had it, Coach."

"Nope. I couldn't make it too easy, right? I'm not saying anything's wrong. It's a great start, but it needs more. If we talk it out like you did with Sam, the answer might pop up again."

"Got any ideas?" asked Marcus.

"Remember when you moved to linebacker?"

"Sure," replied Marcus. "Best move ever. I wouldn't have played in the pros if I didn't."

"I don't remember it so positively," smiled Brian. "I recall you not wanting to move and making our lives miserable."

"Yeah, I guess I did. What's your point?"

"My point is that Charlie didn't only inspire you after his death," continued Brian. "He made you a better player while he was alive too. He spent time with you and JJ not because the coaches asked him to, but because he wanted to. He didn't do it to make *himself* better . . . he did it to make the *team* better."

"Not many people like Charlie."

"No," agreed Brian, "and because of him, there weren't many linebacking corps like the 'Three Musketeers.' That's the team part of Cor Unum I'm talking about."

Marcus nodded.

"Maybe another Latin lesson will help," smiled Brian. "You've heard *E Pluribus Unum*, right? Know what that means?"

"I've seen in on coins, but since I know *Unum* means 'one'; it's not 'In God We Trust,' right?"

"Nope," answered Brian. "E Pluribus Unum was a motto created during our country's early history. When the original 13 colonies were battling, that motto reminded them that in order to be a great team, 'out of many, comes one.' That motto made us one nation."

"I never knew," said Marcus.

"Few do, but that's not the point. My point is you have 100 hearts on this team and the hearts of your staff too. Your job's to connect those hearts and get them beating as one."

"I love it, Coach!" exclaimed Marcus. "So Cor Unum isn't only doing your best; it's also doing your best for the team?"

"Yes," said Brian, "Cor Unum symbolizes the difference between mediocre and great teams . . . *alignment*."

"Alignment?"

"Yes," answered Brian. "The best teams don't always have the best players. I've lost with great players and won with lesser talent. The secret wasn't a few guys buying into my philosophy – *success came when they all did*. When everyone was aligned with our goals and each other, the best teams emerged. And the 'Three Musketeers' were the ultimate example."

"Really?"

"You tell me," replied Brian. "When you played with Charlie and JJ, did you tell them what to do?"

"No," replied Marcus.

"Did you wonder where one of them would be on the field?"

"No."

"Were you ever worried they'd give a half-ass effort?"

"Never."

"That's because you three were aligned in body, mind, and spirit," said Brian. "You were a unit. You acted as one. You were three great players, but played with *one heart*."

"All for one, one for all," smiled Marcus.

"That's what Cor Unum's about," said Brian. "Yes, it's a reminder not to take anything for granted and do your best, but also never to forget the team comes first."

"I like this motto even more."

"We're not finished," said Brian. "You've got more work."

"I was afraid of that," smiled Marcus. "What else is there?"

"To continue developing the Cor Unum philosophy, you must precisely understand what Cor Unum means to you. Write down ideas over the holidays. Once you have your ideas, condense them into your clearest explanation. Then every coach and player must be aligned with what it means for them and the team."

"Okay," said Marcus. "How do I do that?"

"A little more Latin can help with the alignment process," said Brian.

Marcus sat waiting.

"Even though you may understand the motto, that doesn't mean the team does. Cor Unum needs to be a *conspiracy*."

"Conspiracy?" repeated Marcus. "Isn't that a bad thing?"

"No, although many think that way. When people hear 'conspiracy,' they imagine some secret plot to do something illegal, but the word's Latin origins will change that."

"Do tell," smiled Marcus.

"The word 'conspiracy' comes from two Latin words – *con*, meaning 'together,' and *spiro*, meaning 'to breathe.' So, conspiracy is the alignment of a group – everyone breathing together about something."

"Wow," said Marcus, "sounds similar to Cor Unum."

"Yes," replied Brian, "now that you understand what 'conspiracy' means, you need to create one around your Cor Unum philosophy. Instead of using your conspiracy for evil, use yours for good – overthrow the current losing streak of the school. Use Cor Unum as nonstop, positive propaganda until they've heard it so often and understand it so well, they all breathe together."

"Roger," replied Marcus. "I don't want empty words. I want Cor Unum to mean something. Something the team can rally around. I have ideas like T-shirts and talking to Gunny. He'll incorporate Cor Unum into the training too."

"Sounds like your conspiracy's off and running," winked Brian. "Weave the motto into every aspect of this program. With that repetition, Cor Unum will direct the behaviors you want. Speaking of direction, I brought you a gift too."

Marcus opened it, and saw a brown wooden box.

"Remove the lid," Brian instructed.

Marcus found a compass. "Wow. Thanks, Coach. Is it old?"

"It was my father's. But I want you to have it."

"I'm honored," said Marcus.

"I never told you," began Brian, "but my dad always had boats. It's said the two best days for a boat owner are the day you buy it and the day you sell it, but for my dad, that wasn't true. As he got older, the boat sat in our backyard. When he finally sold it, he couldn't get rid of that compass. When he gave it to me, he said when life presented me with 'stormy seas,' I should let the compass guide my 'true north.' You have rough seas ahead, Marcus. Because this job isn't easy, it might seem easier to compromise your values. Let this compass remind you to stay the course."

"I appreciate it, Coach. Thank you."

"Thank me by doing a great job," smiled Brian. "Take advantage of the upcoming free time. It's time this team starts winning."

"About the team," said Marcus, "here's present number two. Almost as good as the Spam."

It was an official team parka.

"Since you're part of this conspiracy, you should look the part. Can't have you around here in that old coat."

"This is great," said Brian, trying it on. "Warm too."

"Looks great on you, Coach." Marcus smiled. "Before you go, I've got one last thing about Cor Unum to share."

"What's that?"

"When I told Sam about 'Every rep, every set,' I said it began with a wake-up call – Charlie's death. I didn't tell him you were the one who called me out. I wanted you to know you turned my life around that day . . . and Cor Unum started with you."

14

Selective Detective

"Welcome back," said Sam.

"Great to be back," replied Brian. "You don't meet me downstairs by the car anymore?"

"Ha! I was testing if you remembered how to get up here."

"I found it," Brian smiled, "and I'll be grading you on some tests today too!"

"I look forward to it," said Sam. "How was your holiday?"

"I had a great time with my family. My daughters and their families visited, and it was nice to have the house filled again. Filling my stomach was another matter. I need to work off a few pounds. I blame the grandkids, though. You'll see someday – a grandfather's job is easy. Make the kids laugh, and give them back to their parents if there's a problem."

"I have to worry about kids before grandkids, right? Isn't that how it works?"

"Yes, that's still the order," Brian smirked. "How was your holiday?"

"Since Melissa and I hadn't planned anything, we booked a last-minute trip. We found a Caribbean cruise deal we couldn't pass up! We always talked about a cruise, so we were spontaneous and booked it. We did the 'see the parents' thing for Christmas, then flew to Florida and spent seven days on the boat."

"Wow," said Brian. "I heard the food's amazing."

"Amazing and nonstop! There was always some-thing delicious to eat. Melissa and I had to ration our-selves. We visited four different islands too. The trip was never 'relaxing,' but that's not our style. I noticed the stress she's under. She kept getting on the computer, but even with that irritation, we talked about our careers and relationship. Next time we have challenges, I'll just trap my wife on a boat. Then she has to talk to me!"

"Great!" smiled Brian. "Like I said, culture starts at home. And because communication's critical for culture, make sure it happens regularly. As you experienced, a leader needs to recharge the batteries too. Working nonstop seems the way to do more, but it can be counterproductive and burn you out. I always returned from vacations recharged and inspired. As your culture coach, I'm prescribing a couple trips a year with some weekend adventures thrown in too."

"Melissa won't have problems filling that script. I took this too," Sam said, holding up his notebook. "Every night, I journaled about Stamina's three Bs. I also wrote about my vision, values, and leadership role."

"That's putting it to good use," replied Brian.

On Sam's desk, Brian noticed different garments.

"I want to show you these," Sam said, pointing to the assortment of shirts and hats. "Dana's taken charge of your 'uniform' idea. She sought out vendors, found the ones with the best prices, and these are the final choices. We're deciding what to give out."

"Looks like nice stuff. Cool gear can be great for building team spirit," Brian said. "What's this?"

"Ahh, those are the Stamina bowling jerseys! I asked Raj about social outings we could try. He said the engineers had a team in a bowling league, and there was another one starting up. So, after the New Year, we took the group bowling. Afterward we asked who'd like join a league and got almost a hundred percent commitment."

"Sounds fun," said Brian. "and seems like you're following the treatment plan. You've worked on my uniform and language ideas, and have Group Therapy going. How's the 'bread breaking?'"

"That has been your best lesson. I can't believe how I disconnected by hiding in my office. Now my schedule's available for three lunches a week. A person can book the time they want and so everyone gets an opportunity, you can't book more than one lunch per month. So while breaking bread with 12 people a month, I hear their ideas and get to know them better. I've already learned things I never knew."

"*No contact, no culture*," said Brian. "Staying in touch with your people's important. Since you're opening lines of communication here, what about the people who work remotely?"

"That's been more challenging. Working remotely lets my business leverage people from a wider area, but that distance hurts the culture here. I've reached out and set up Zoom calls. I've also invited those in the area to the lunch schedule and bowling too. Since the workplace has changed, I'm still figuring it out."

"Good work," said Brian. "The leader's job is to find solutions as things change. And things will change. Your job's no longer to write programs; it's to program the mission into your people. I like the transition you're making from 'technician' to leader. You've grown and I'm proud of you."

Sam sat back and smiled.

"You've made big strides," Brian continued, "but there's still further to go."

"Ready when you are," replied Sam.

"Good," said Brian. "My original lessons taught you to identify and clarify Stamina's three Bs. Since you've started to establish them, it's time to learn how to support and reinforce your culture. Your culture will require constant nurturing. With proper nurturing, your culture will prosper. But just a little neglect could destroy it."

"I feel good about the first two Bs," replied Sam. "I've categorized my Beings and have meetings in place. I've also clarified Stamina's Beliefs and have shared my vision and values. But for Behaviors, as I'm examining the 'white space' for rituals, I'm still unclear."

"Seems like a mystery, right?" Brian smiled. "That's what I'll cover today. You know the three Bs, but to create and reinforce them, you'll need the six As!"

"You've got culture figured out, don't you?"

"Spend 40 years on something and you'll solve most mysteries, kid," smiled Brian. "My ideas may appear simple, but when you hired me, you didn't purchase just my knowledge – you purchased my pain. It looks like I have things figured out, but it took a long time. By following my lessons, you won't make 40 years of mistakes like I did."

"Hindsight's 20/20, huh?"

"Absolutely," nodded Brian. "And to use the six As correctly, you'll need your sight again. My job started with making you aware of culture by looking into the 'white space.' Now that you see it and recognize it's under your control, it's time to use a magnifying glass and get more focused. Instead of a tech guy, you must think like a sleuth – like a *Selective Detective*."

"Cool!" exclaimed Sam. "I like puzzles, so maybe I'll enjoy cracking the case of Stamina's culture."

"Good. As a Selective Detective you'll do what a detective does – be on the lookout for evidence . . . evidence of things that either promote or destroy your culture. Once you've developed your detective skills, then the six As will help make sure Stamina's story doesn't become a murder mystery."

"I'll keep my eyes out for Vultures and wakes," smiled Sam.

Brian smirked.

"Okay," started Sam, "how do I look for evidence?"

"It's pretty straightforward. You walk the office watching your Being's Behaviors and compare them to Stamina's Beliefs. Use your magnifying glass and compare people's actions to the culture you want. Depending on the clues you find, you'll know which of the six As to use."

"So what are they?" asked Sam.

"Let me explain," said Brian. "Every interaction here is a *Cultural Exchange*. And each of those exchanges either supports or defeats your culture. Depending on which of the three Bs is affected, you get two choices how to handle an exchange. One choice promotes your culture and the other destroys it. The six As, therefore, get you closer to or further from the culture you desire."

Sam wrote a note and said, "So as a Selective Detective, I'm examining every exchange and comparing it to my perfect picture of culture?"

"Yes," nodded Brian. "Then you choose your response. And that response chooses your culture."

"Wow. You've made it easy."

"Don't get too excited, kid," Brian warned. "Easy things are easy not to do. Knowledge doesn't guarantee action. Look at your current situation. You knew Stamina had a cultural problem and chose to do nothing. That choice made things worse. The three Bs are about knowledge and the six As are about the consequences of choosing to take an action or not."

"Haven't I been an action-taker?"

"For sure," replied Brian. "Sorry for the suspense, but it's a mystery, right? Last thing about the six As – once you start using them, the ultimate goal is for your staff to use them too. But that won't happen until you do it first. As a Selective Detective, look at everything as a cultural exchange and make the decision whether it's positive or negative. People are often better at seeing the negative things, but remember, the faster way to build your culture is by seeing the positive."

"Fair enough."

"To write these down," continued Brian, "place two of the six As under 'Beings,' two under Behaviors, and two under Beliefs. Each of those two represent a choice."

Sam made the notes.

"Now you're ready. The two As under 'Beings' are *Address* and *Avoid*. As a Selective Detective, you'll see exchanges where your Beings either say, do, or interact in a way you do or don't want. When that happens, it's your choice to either address or avoid that Being. For both positive and negative exchanges, you'll use the power of *recognition* to direct your culture. So, if Dana did something good and you addressed her, you increase the chances her action will become part of your culture. But if you avoid her, even though she did something good, best case she never knows it, and worst case her resentment has a negative effect. And when someone does something you don't want, you're still required to address or avoid. For instance, if Raj behaved in a way you didn't like, you can address him and stop the behavior, or avoid him. If you chose avoid, you'll see more bad behavior in the future."

Sam said, "My style's more avoid than address. And even when I addressed things, I didn't reinforce it well."

"That's a common leadership problem," said Brian. "Confrontation's never easy and most people avoid it. By committing to *lead* this company, you must do the tough tasks. Whenever I addressed an uncomfortable situation, I'd use the definitions of the three Bs to assist. For instance, the definition of Beings is 'who we are.' When I saw something I liked, I said, 'That's who we are here.' If I saw something I didn't like, I said, 'That's not who we are here.' Even with that trick, it was still tough, but the more you address things, the easier it gets."

"I hope so. I've got things I don't want to address."

"Do what others don't do and you'll get what others don't got," smiled Brian. "Look, it's easier to talk about this than do it. But using the definitions of the three Bs to guide you helps. Ready for the next two As?"

"Yes."

"Okay," started Brian, "the first two As recognize the power of recognition. So, the actions of your Beings are guided by whatever you address or avoid. Those actions become their Behaviors, which eventually become your culture's rituals. Your culture will rise or fall to the level of the behaviors you *tolerate*. That tolerance is covered by the next two As – *Allow* and *Admonish*."

Sam wrote them down.

"When you address your Beings, the most common thing you'll address are their behaviors. Allowing or admonishing behaviors is how you build and maintain your culture. Using my trick, since Behaviors are 'how we do it,' when you see something you allow, say, 'That's how we do it.'' And when you see something to admonish, say, 'That's not how we do it,'' and explain why. This way, everyone learns whether a behavior is or isn't acceptable."

As Sam wrote, he said, "I see how these simple actions define and drive a culture . . . and they're misused here."

"Not just here," replied Brian. "The six As are misused in most businesses. That's why most businesses don't last. The final two As deal with something lasting – your Beliefs. Although technology can change quickly, Stamina's values shouldn't. Another thing you'll commonly address is whether Behaviors support or violate Stamina's Beliefs. The two As to write are *Advocate* and *Arraign*."

Sam wrote those down too.

"When you advocate something, you publicly support it and everyone knows where you stand. When you arraign something, instead of support, you find fault. Your Beliefs are 'what we stand for,' and again using my trick, if you see something supporting your values, say, 'That's what we stand for.' And when someone violates the values, arraign them by saying, 'That's not what we stand for.'"

Sam continued note taking.

"These expose holes in my leadership," Sam began. "I knew something was wrong and chose to do nothing. Part of my inaction was due to fear, but, in my defense, I didn't know what to do. This is the blueprint I needed."

"Fear is normal," smiled Brian. "Before you had no one to guide you. Now you're in detective school. This afternoon, we'll walk the floor and I'll point out how I'd use the six As. And you'll get practice."

"That'll help."

"Before I forget," Brian said scanning the apparel, "after seeing this gear, make sure you aren't forgetting someone."

"If you wanted a shirt, you just had to ask."

"Not for me, Sam," laughed Brian. "You're forgetting one of the five steps of my treatment plan."

"I thought we covered them all?"

"Nope," answered Brian.

"Who'd I forget?" Sam asked.

"This should explain. When I was a young coach, I'd attend coaching clinics to hear famous coaches speak. Although the lectures were great, I learned more at the social afterward. As young coaches networked, the older coaches held court. At one clinic, I met a very famous coach. Because this living legend had a couple Super Bowl rings, most coaches were afraid to ask him anything. Because I was young, I pulled a rookie move and asked the 'secret question.'"

"The secret question?" asked Sam.

"Yessir. I said, 'Hey Coach, what's your secret?' That classic, vague, and open-ended question usually gets a young coach slapped. But instead of ignoring me, he said two words I hadn't heard before. . . ."

"What'd he say?"

"He said," responded Brian, "don't forget *Unspoken Tokens*."

"Wait a minute," said Sam, "Selective Detectives and Unspoken Tokens? A lot of rhyming today, huh?"

"You remembered them, didn't you? His words, not mine. You wanna learn what they mean?"

"Of course," answered Sam.

"As he was building his championship organization, the coach realized his players were occasionally distracted or distressed from problems at home. This proved how influential the players' families were, and the importance of making those people feel part of the team. So, after big victories, instead of the players, he gave gifts to their wives and children. He didn't go cheap either. The bigger the victory, the greater the gift. One year was jewelry and another brand-new TVs. But regardless of the gift, they were accompanied by a hand-written card recognizing their importance. Since NFL games are decided by a few points, the coach said these Unspoken Tokens made the difference."

"Now I get it," replied Sam. "I remembered my culture at home but forgot my 30 people have 30 families too."

"Yes, and those people influence the ethic and attitude of your people. Since you're getting gear, don't exclude their families – include them. The more those families feel part of Stamina, the more supportive they'll be. It could become the secret behind your greatest victories too."

"Another great morning," said Sam. "Wanna get lunch and a plan for this afternoon's detective work?"

"I'm always up for breaking bread, kid."

15

Cor Unum

"Everyone in!" yelled Marcus across the indoor practice field.

As his players huddled around him, Marcus shouted, "Take a knee."

Once everyone was silent, he began.

"Welcome back and to a new year." Marcus began. "This time can inspire you to leave old things behind . . . but it also causes insecurity looking toward new things ahead. My goal today is to remove any of the fears or doubts you might have about our future."

Marcus paused.

"I won't be the coach keeping secrets from you. And one thing that's no secret is we must win this season! I wouldn't have taken this job if I didn't think we could do it. You may be worried I have a rebuilding plan . . . you know . . . bring in my own players, sit the veterans, and give myself three years to have a winning season. Well," Marcus raised his voice, "stop worrying about that! This isn't a *rebuild* – this is a *return*! You probably chose to play here, just like I did, because of the history and tradition of this school. That tradition's about a lot of things, but it's mainly about winning. We're not rebuilding . . . we're returning to that tradition right now!"

The players were nodding.

"I've watched the film. We've got players here – and we can win this season. Most of you were four-star kids from somewhere, right? From what I've seen, the talent was always here; you just weren't putting it together. Because it's a new year, I want us imagining the future, not pointing fingers at the past. I've heard about your last coach. This is the first and last time I want him mentioned. I'm the head coach now, and I promise – unlike your last coach, you'll see me everywhere!

143

"I'll be at the training table. In study hall. I'll drop in on workouts too. But Gunny has it covered until I get you in March," Marcus continued, pointing at Gunny. "As for Coach Gunderson, and all the coaches I've brought in, they have my total support. They've been brought here because I believe they'll give us the best chance to win now. If you have a new position coach you haven't met yet, start building a relationship, because this ship's leaving and you don't want to miss it."

"Relationships," Marcus continued, "are built on trust. I know I'll need to earn yours. Relationships take time to create and I will spend that time. You want to meet? Let me know. You have something to share? Let me know! There's nothing more important to me. I'm a coach who doesn't have my best interests in mind . . ." Marcus paused.

"I have *our* best interests in mind!" Marcus yelled.

"To explain, I have a football story. There was once a talented football player. This guy always made the highlight reel. He had it all – the stats, the media coverage, and the girl too. But one thing always upset him. After returning to his alma mater, he met with his coach to discuss it. He told his coach that although he'd been All-Conference, he was confused why he was never team captain. He also mentioned he resented his best friend because he'd been elected captain multiple times. His jealousy for his friend bothered him. These feelings brought him back to find out why he was never selected.

"Then," continued Marcus, "his coach told him something that changed his life. He told the star player, 'You're one of the best players I've ever coached. Your friend didn't possess your talent, but he was named captain because of something different. He said that you were the best player *on* the team, but he was the best player *for* the team. . . . Why am I telling you this? *Because I was that star player.* . . .

"Why I came back to find out the answer," Marcus continued, "was because my best friend and team captain, Charlie Powell, died in a tragic accident right after we were drafted to the NFL. I was so upset I thought about quitting. But my coach, Coach Knight, convinced me the best way to honor him was by being a player like him. What I heard that day was not easy to accept, but Coach was right – I wanted to be the best player in the country, while Charlie wanted us to be the best team in the country."

Marcus choked up. No one moved.

"What I learned changed me as a player and a person. When I started in the pros, I adopted a new philosophy. I wish I could say I was All-Pro and had a Hall of Fame career, but I can't. But due to that philosophy, I'm proud to say I was elected captain of two different NFL teams. I don't say that to impress you, but to impress upon you that it took many years of playing to figure it out. You've been on teams your whole life. But that doesn't mean you were taught to be a good teammate. Part of my job's to make you a better football player, but I also want to make you a better team player. This spring, we'll spend time putting in our offensive and defensive plans. But for the next few months of speed and strength training, I want to input our philosophical plan. That philosophy's rooted in one idea – it's better to be the best person *for* the team than the best person *on* the team."

Marcus pointed to his gold wristband and said, "And the 'war cry' of that philosophy will be two words . . . Cor Unum."

The players were riveted.

"Every one of you brings a beating heart to this team. If your focus is being the best on the team, your heart will beat by itself. My goal is to get all your hearts beating as one. *Cor Unum* is Latin for 'one heart.'"

A few players smiled.

"When my friend passed, I played like every game was my last. I left everything on the field, and never took another play for granted. I applied that mindset to every aspect of my life – I trained, ate, and slept like it was the most important thing in the world. I realized for the big things to happen, I had to do the littlest things perfectly . . . down to every thought I had, breath I took, and beat of my one heart. Part of what Cor Unum represents is what my friend reminded me – you only get so many beats, so make every one count!"

Marcus composed himself.

"But," said Marcus, holding up his left hand, "in addition to making everything count, there are five other things Cor Unum represents. These will be the core values of our team. If you live up to these values, you'll be a better team player and person. Live up to them, or you won't play here. Soon you'll see these five words everywhere – in the locker room, the weight room, and meeting rooms. Today I wanted to explain them so there's no doubt what they mean to me."

"Number one," said Marcus pointing his index finger, "is *Excelsior*. That word means 'ever upward.' This team must rise up, and this value demands you take nothing for granted. This season I'll demand your best. Excelsior is our reminder we may never achieve perfection, but we must pursue excellence."

Marcus held up his index and middle finger.

"Number two is *Ambition*. This word represents a strong desire to achieve. Without Ambition, Excelsior is hard to carry out over a long season. With ambition fueling your desire to win, hard work becomes easy."

Then Marcus held up three fingers.

"Number three is *Respect*. Everyone counts on this team. Respect requires you to appreciate everyone for their talents and what they bring to the team. Starters are not more important than backups. Running backs don't score without O-linemen. We don't win if the defense can't hold our opponent to fewer points. We won't tolerate jealousy or envy. And we won't only respect players here. Our coaches, training staff, and anyone involved with this team is important and will be treated as such."

Marcus held up four fingers and said, "Number four's *Trust*. Trust allows the whole world to operate, and we'll have it here. With trust, we can hold each other accountable. Like I mentioned, Trust takes time to build, but it'll be worth it."

"And Trust is the glue that'll hold us together when things get tough. You must live up to those four values *on* this team. But in order for this philosophy to exert its true power, we all need to live them *for* this team. That's why the final value," as he pointed his right index finger at his left thumb, "is *Harmony*."

"You may recognize the word from music. When a number of voices come together, they create something different. We'll be the best for the team by staying harmonious in our values, goals, and purpose – united in our knowledge and skills because united we'll win or divided we'll fall. I don't want a team of 100 hearts beating . . ." said Marcus closing his thumb around his fist and bringing it over his chest, "I want a team of 100 with one beating heart . . . Cor Unum." Marcus beat his fist against his chest, mimicking a heartbeat.

The players were nodding.

"As you'll notice," said Marcus, pointing at his gold wristband, "this Cor Unum band has an acronym on it – *H.E.A.R.T.* H for Harmony. E for Excelsior. A for Ambition. R for Respect, and T for Trust. There's only one heart on this band. . . . Do you think you can you remember that?"

Players shouted, "Yes, sir!"

"These bands aren't given," shouted Marcus. "They're earned. And the keeper of these bands is Coach Gunderson. Before I hand you off to Gunny, I'll make one more promise – This philosophy isn't going away. I won't play the 11 best on the team . . . it'll be the 11 who are the best for the team. The 11 who play with one heart."

Marcus scanned the group.

"Gunny, they're all yours," said Marcus, and he left the field.

Gunny – 240 pounds of muscle and bone – surveyed the players like an artisan examines his raw materials. His voice was weathered from decades of abuse.

"Okay, men," began Gunny, "I hope you enjoyed that. I've been around Coach Chase for a long time, and we couldn't be more excited to take on this challenge. Over break, you should've gotten a training packet. I hope you read it and performed the workouts. By the end of today, I'll know if you didn't."

His last statement had players nervous.

"These next few months, we'll be *training* together. Notice I said 'training' and not 'working out' or 'exercising.' It's important you understand the difference. To me, 'training' means following a plan to reach a goal. When you're training, nothing's left to chance and everything has purpose. Exercising or working out is a random series of movements or workouts. There'll be nothing random here. That's not how victories happen. I'll have a reason behind everything, and if you want to know it, just ask. Everything we'll do is designed to make you the strongest, fastest, and toughest version of yourself. I'm not here to make you tired or use exercises for the sake of looking cool. My goal is to help you reach your potential and give this team the best chance to win."

Gunny paused.

"During our winter training, we'll spend a lot of time doing traditional lifts and sprints. You may consider bench presses, squats, and 40-yard dashes 'ordinary.' I believe success results from doing ordinary things extraordinarily well. So, it doesn't matter *if* you bench press; it matters *how* you bench press. I don't care *if* you sprint; I care *how* you sprint. We only get eight hours a week, and I'm going to make them count.

Gunny continued as assistant coaches began placing cones on the field.

"My program won't include anything new – just greater attention to detail. But there is something unique to my programming. In addition to periodic testing of maxes and sprint times, I'm going to put you through physical and mental challenges called *Cauldrons* . . . and today you'll try one. When you hear the word 'cauldron,' you may imagine a metal pot and open fire, but the word also represents a situation characterized by agitation, instability, and strong emotions. So, my Cauldrons are challenges designed to push your individual limits and, according to Cor Unum, get you to work together as a team. They won't seem fun at the time, but you'll be thankful for what the Cauldrons force you to become."

Gunny then yelled, "Everybody up!"

"Every training session involves my specific warmup. This warmup will start everything we do. We'll use it during weight sessions, sprint sessions, and games. Today I'm going to teach you to do it right. If you're going to be warming up in front of 70,000 people in nine months, we need to start performing it perfectly now. That's what Coach meant by the word *Excelsior*. How you do one thing is how you do everything!" yelled Gunny. "When you do this warmup great, you'll be ready to do the next thing great. I will explain how I want things done today. Your job's to do the best you can. If it can be better, I'll let you know. Is everyone ready to warm up?"

"Yes sir!" answered the team.

Using very specific commands and detailed demonstration, Gunny spent an hour teaching a warmup that would eventually be performed in 15 minutes.

"Okay men," Gunny began, "today Coach Chase introduced you to Cor Unum, which means 'one heart.' Now that we're warmed up, we're going to throw you in the Cauldron and test where your heart's at. As you may have figured out from these cones, today we're doing a sprint test. It might seem like it tests cardio, but I'm testing your mind too. Today's Cauldron is the 'Beep Test.'"

Some of the players groaned.

"Sounds like some of you are familiar with it. For those who aren't, the beep test's a test of your cardiovascular ability. But as you'll learn, it tests your heart and your fighting spirit. When athletes quit this test, most don't stop for physical reasons; they give up because of a weak fighting spirit. Over the next three months, I'm going to strengthen that spirit. I don't want you to come to 'practice,' I want you to *come to fight*! Today's your chance to earn your Cor Unum band and show how much 'heart' you've got!"

16

Trophy Case

"Come on in," said Brian.

"Good to see you," replied Sam, walking into Brian's house. "Thanks for having me. You tired of driving over to Stamina?"

"Ha! We've spent a lot of time in your office. It's time you saw mine."

"Beautiful neighborhood," said Sam. "Have you lived here long?"

"I've been in the area for 30 years. But we had other houses before this one. It's too big for just me now, but there's no way I could sell it. Let me show you around."

Brian showed Sam the first floor and the upstairs bedrooms where his daughters had returned over the holidays. Then they went to the kitchen and sat down.

"Want something to drink?" Brian asked.

"Sure," replied Sam. "What do you have?"

"I have milk, OJ, and flavored seltzers if you're interested."

"I'll try one," said Sam.

"Be careful. Coach Chase got me on these – they take getting used to."

Sam took a sip and gritted his teeth.

"Told you," smiled Brian. "At least it's carbonated. I pretend they taste good."

"Yeah," agreed Sam, "those would take getting used to."

"Before I show you the rest of the house, how's Stamina? Your email updates have been great."

"Thanks," replied Sam. "And your responses have helped. I'll need another notebook soon. Mine's half full."

"That can be arranged. So what do you have to report?"

"Overall," began Sam, "by being a 'Selective Detective,' I've found evidence of improvement. Since we last met, we've distributed the Stamina gear and it was a hit. People are wearing the clothes and Dana will pick a new item quarterly. We picked an 'Unspoken Token' for family members too! Dana's using the 12th man idea with her customer service team. When a service rep goes the extra mile, they call it 'pulling a 12.'"

"Ha!" chuckled Brian. "I like it, and her. Told you she was a star."

"Uh-huh," continued Sam, "and the best news is she's staying on board! And the clothes people are on board with most are the bowling shirts. That league's connected our group. Even though we're not the best bowlers, it launched a new Stamina ritual."

"Oh yeah? What's that?"

"It started with Shelly," began Sam. "She may be our worst bowler, but she's the best at cheering for others. Whenever someone got a strike or spare, she'd give them a high five. And not the one-handed version – Shelly throws a double-handed version. After a few weeks, her teammates started doing it. Then the other day, I saw Raj give that high five to another engineer! Speaking of Raj, he's creating a game for Coach Chase you'll love."

"Sounds like you've got a virus going on."

"Virus?" asked Sam.

"Yes," Brian replied. "Everyone celebrating together in a social setting has started a positivity virus. As you've noticed, it's contagious."

"Yeah, but not everything's positive. . . ."

"What's up?" asked Brian.

"Following the treatment plan, we've had group meetings too," Sam began. "And not only individual team meetings; I've held meetings with the entire staff. Instead of helping, things got heated."

"Like heated how?"

"Well," continued Sam, "I've seen different types of 'entitlement' shining through. For instance, the engineers look down on everyone because they create the programs. And the sales team thinks they should run Stamina since they generate the money. I want everyone working together, but when we do, there's friction."

"I understand," said Brian. "Friction isn't only normal; it can also lead to great things. You're not the only computer guy who didn't understand that."

"Who are you talking about?"

"Ahh," began Brian, "you might've heard of him. His computer company made a dent in the universe."

"Steve Jobs?" asked Sam. "Yeah, some vision, huh? I like that I have something in common with him . . . what is it?"

"When Steve Jobs started running Apple, he used a 'my-way-or-the-highway' style of leadership. That led to little collaboration between his people. Whether that was the main reason or not, he was fired from his own company."

"That I did know," answered Sam.

"What you might not know," continued Brian, "is that Jobs had an older neighbor for a mentor. After he lost his company, he remembered a lesson this man taught him years earlier. The old man showed Jobs a rock tumbler. He had Jobs pick out some rocks and place them in the tumbler. A few days later, Jobs returned to find those average rocks looking like polished gemstones. Jobs realized he'd never made Apple like that rock tumbler.

He would have been a better leader getting his people to bump together and polish each other more."

"Wow. That's a great analogy."

"It's also a testament for the positive side of *friction*," said Brian. "Jobs didn't make the same mistake twice. At his second company, he built an area where everyone was forced to come in contact with each other, where they could bump ideas and battle for them. Above that space he placed a crest stating, *Alienus Non Dietius*, which means, 'Alone no longer.'"

Sam wrote and said, "So friction isn't so bad after all?"

"I'd say it's necessary! Be more worried when no one has any opposing ideas. Yeah, friction may have made a lot of noise at Jobs's second company, but they made people happy . . . and rich too. Maybe you've heard of it? It's called Pixar."

"Lesson taken," said Sam. "So is all friction positive?"

"Good question. Although friction can be positive, that doesn't mean it's always good. Friction can polish your people, but it can also grind them down."

"I know what you mean," sighed Sam. "One person is grinding on all of us."

"Let me guess . . ." said Brian, "Rick?"

"Right again." Sam slumped. "He's becoming the biggest problem at Stamina. He's resistant at our group meetings, and from my individual meetings, I've received negative feedback about him."

"So what's your plan?"

"It's a tough situation," answered Sam. "Rick's a close friend and Stamina's first hire. I like him as a person, but he's using that friendship to hold me hostage. But besides our friendship, as Head of Sales, he's runs the division responsible for bringing in the money."

"You're in a tough position," said Brian. "Mixing personal and business relationships isn't always easy. In fact, sometimes one can destroy the other."

"He acts like he owns the business," continued Sam, "even though he's never put in his own money. He had the chance and not taking it surprised me. And when I pin him down about his job, I get the runaround. I'm wondering what Stamina would be like without him, but I'm afraid to lose that money."

"In business and life," Brian began, "people rise to their level of incompetence. As you grow, you're faced with new challenges. If you pass them, you move to the next level – if you don't, you stay there. Rick's risen to his highest level and unfortunately either he doesn't want to do more work or have the talent to go further. Whether it's a lack of desire or talent, it's a perfect reason to teach you a math formula related to culture."

"A math formula?"

"Yes," replied Brian, "and because of your fears, it'll take courage and trust to use it. Many leaders don't have the guts to use this formula, and suffer much longer than they have to."

"What's the formula?"

"*Addition by subtraction*," Brian said.

Sam wrote down the words.

"Everyone at Stamina is replaceable, Sam – even you. Even though your instinct says Rick should go, you're fearful because of the money he generates and your friendship. Your anxiety's created by worrying what might get subtracted from Stamina if you remove him. But things can be added to a culture when someone hurting that culture is removed. Instead of worrying what negatives might happen if he goes, imagine the positives – like who might rise to a new level or what developments might happen when you remove his friction."

"I never thought like that," admitted Sam. "You're right about my fear and anxiety. This has bothered me for months, and I'm disappointed in my lack of courage to address it."

"This stuff isn't easy," said Brian. "And nothing has to happen immediately. I suggest meeting with Rick to clear the air. Let him know how you feel and find out more about what he's doing at Stamina. After that, you'll know what to do. And here's more wisdom from Steve Jobs that might help."

"What's that?"

"If you want to make everyone happy, don't be a leader. Sell ice cream." replied Brian.

"Yes. It's always great talking with you. Where'd you learn everything?"

"Glad you asked," said Brian. "Some is experience, but most of what I've learned came from downstairs. Let's go see."

Brian led Sam downstairs. On the left Sam saw a half-dozen bookshelves filled with books. On the right were bookcases filled with sports awards. Sam walked to the trophy case first. As Sam looked over the plaques, rings, and medals, Brian noticed that he seemed to be particularly interested in the team photos. He moved from one to the next as if he were looking for something. When he didn't seem to find it, he said, "You've got lots of awards here."

"Ahh," replied Brian, "those are great, but you can't see the work it took to get them. And some are just awards for getting awards."

"But it's impressive," Sam said. "You must be proud of it."

"Of course I am, kid. But as you get older, you'll learn it's not about the trophies. Ever heard of John Baker?"

"No," said Sam. "Who's that?"

"John Baker was a runner from Albuquerque," began Brian, "but his running began by accident. His high school track coach wanted John's best friend on the team. Since the friend would only join if John did, John started running. At the first cross country meet, John shocked everyone and set the course record! After that, he won race after race and by 18 years old, he was one of the nation's best milers."

Brian looked at his trophies.

"John went to the University of New Mexico, and because he kept beating top runners, they called him 'Upset John.' Well, 'Upset John' led his team to upset victories over the greatest schools. When college ended, he set his sights on the 1972 Olympics. To pay for his training, he took a job teaching at Aspen Elementary School. The kids loved John and he became the school's most popular teacher.

"Right before his 25th birthday," Brian continued, "John began having trouble getting through workouts. A painful and swollen mass developed in his groin. The doctors had the worst news; John had advanced testicular cancer and was given six months to live."

Brian bowed his head. "John had surgeries but they didn't help. One night in despair, John drove to the top of a mountain and thought about taking his life. Then he thought about his students at Aspen Elementary and could not imagine letting these kids down. That moment, he dedicated himself to those students, and went back to teaching."

Brian picked a medal from the shelf.

"John started a track team. After every practice and meet, John would give out awards to the fastest runners who, even in defeat, never gave up. Each day he'd hand out another trophy and the kids worked harder. John's health deteriorated, but he pressed on because his team qualified for the national championships. Unfortunately, John passed before the meet, but his team was inspired and won the national title."

Brian looked at the medal in his hand.

"Months later, two interesting things happened. The first was the families of Aspen Elementary petitioned to change the school's name to John Baker Elementary. After 520 families voted, the final count was 520 to none. The second thing involved the trophies John had handed out. When the kids showed them to John's family, they realized they were John's medals with his name removed from them."

Brian handed the medal to Sam.

Sam said, "Wow, that puts things into perspective. Thanks."

"You can thank me by learning that *success and significance* are two different things. Let me show you my real trophy case," Brian said as he pointed at the books. "You asked where I learned everything. Well, this is the place."

"Did you read all of these?" asked Sam.

"Every one of them. When I started reading, I developed a system. I wouldn't let myself put a book on my shelf until it'd been read. And if you look in each one, you'll find dog-eared pages and notes of the information I found important. My wife used to tell me I was crazy, but these books tell me my life's pursuits. They're more important than my trophies."

"Wow," replied Sam. "There must be thousands of books here. I'm not a fast reader."

"I wasn't either," said Brian. "I started reading when I got serious about coaching. With practice, I read faster. One book led to another. Then 30 years later, you end up reading a lot of books. I heard if you read four or five books on a subject, you're an expert. I took that idea and ran with it. If you look, I have dozens of subjects represented by more than five books."

"I see sport books, but also finance, history, sales, marketing, and more. And look at this," said Sam pointing at a stack of golden notebooks. "Looks like you have some of those too."

"Certainly," said Brian, "that habit started long ago when an old coach got me started."

"Sounds familiar. Are they filled?"

"Sure are," said Brian, "and of all the books on these shelves, those are my most valuable. Once you read enough about what other people think, it's time to write down your thoughts. My first notebook was about coaching."

"Do you miss coaching?"

"I'm coaching you, aren't I?" joked Brian.

"That's not what I mean. After looking at your awards, do you miss being on the field?"

"Maybe in the beginning," replied Brian, "but now what I miss is giving the greatest gift of coaching."

"What's that?" said Sam.

"When I was head coach," Brian explained, "I'd hang with the exercise science professors. In addition to helping with training ideas for our team, they were cool guys.

One of the teachers had won some national awards. Every year he ranked as one of the top professors at our school. Seeking to get better, I asked him why he was popular. His answer changed my coaching forever."

"What did he say?"

"He said there wasn't anything special about him. He didn't have any knowledge other professors didn't have and he didn't possess any technology you couldn't find at other schools either. His secret was his approach – he had one goal for every lecture, and that goal was to give his students a *memory* they wouldn't forget."

"A memory?" replied Sam, "That's it?"

"That's it?" exclaimed Brian. "Think back to school. Can you remember many days? Do you remember all your classes with a certain teacher?"

"No."

"That's right!" said Brian. "But what about the time you've spent with me? Got any memories?"

"Sure, I have a bunch."

"That's because I'm a coach who puts value in creating memories," replied Brian. "Instead of a mentor; I want to be a 'mentor-tainer.' And instead of boring lessons, I've tried to provide 'mentor-tainment!' Whether it's a story, a video, or some kind of puzzle, I teach in a way you won't forget. Because . . ." Brian continued as he looked at the trophy case, "rings eventually sit in the box, kid. But memories are gifts you use forever. You need to create memories at Stamina. Give out more memories than shirts or hats. Make the days more memorable than your days in school. Most people can't remember days, but they do remember moments. Your job is to create *moments worth remembering*."

"I understand," replied Sam. "I'm trying that with our bowling nights and lunches, but do you think you can make every day memorable?"

"When I was your age, I didn't see a need to make every day special. With so many days ahead, I reserved special moments for when I got older. Well . . ." he said pointing to the golden notebooks, "my first subject was coaching, but the last I wrote about was loss. In particular the loss of my wife. After she passed, my biggest discovery was there are no average days. Every day is and can be memorable. Looking back, a big regret was that it took losing her to learn it. Another was letting so many days together pass without making it memorable. If you viewed your days like I do now, you'd treat them more special. My best advice is, don't wait until the funeral to buy someone you love roses."

"Thanks for sharing that," Sam said. "You've given me memories I won't forget."

"Hmm," nodded Brian. "Thank you too."

"Why?"

"You just reminded me of another benefit from giving a memory. When you give someone a rose, some of the fragrance lingers on your hand too."

17

Helmet Stickers

"Thanks for meeting again, Coach," said Sam as he passed a bagel and coffee to Marcus.

"You get the thanks," said Marcus. "Your Cor Unum has brought this team together!"

"Really?"

"Yes . . . it all started with this band," Marcus said, showing his wristband. "After I finalized what Cor Unum meant, we made bands for the players to earn. We introduced it last month and they've become a badge of honor."

"That's great to hear," said Sam. "How do they earn one?"

"Our strength coach, Gunny," replied Marcus, "uses a tough test called the beep test that players must pass."

"Has everyone passed?"

"Not yet," replied Marcus. "Most have, but the real value isn't if they pass or not – it's what's happening to our culture."

"How so?"

"If you look here," said Marcus, turning the band on his wrist, "in addition to Cor Unum, I added H.E.A.R.T. to the other side. It stands for our five core values – Harmony, Excelsior, Ambition, Respect, and Trust."

"Whoa," said Sam. "That *is* cool."

"Thanks. The players think so too. It's hard to connect with a different generation, but the players love it. Since explaining Cor Unum, they've stepped up. That snowballed into last week's breakthrough."

"What was that?" asked Sam.

"I went to watch players take another crack at earning their band." replied Marcus. "I only expected a few players, but the whole team showed up! And the best part? Most weren't there to retest. They were there to pace and cheer on their teammates! To pass this test, you must complete a certain number of laps, depending on your position. This test's downright torture. As the runners got more tired, the encouragement got louder – until the moment happened. With six laps to go, the other players formed a narrow passage for the players to run between. Every support player was clapping and screaming and each player passed! When they got their bands, their teammates huddled around them celebrating. It was the 'goosebump' moment the culture turned around here . . . all for a rubber band."

"Sounds like things are looking up. And I need a band idea for my company too."

"Well . . ." said Marcus as he pulled out a Cor Unum band, "put this on so you don't forget."

"Wow, Coach. I'm not sure I've earned it. You won't make me run, will you?"

"Nah," replied Marcus smiling. "I didn't run, either. Of all the bands that've been given out, you've earned it the most. By coming up with Cor Unum, you helped change the culture here. Wear that band with pride."

Sam put it on.

"Thanks, Coach. That means a lot. That moment happened just because of this band?"

"The band," Marcus said, "is important, but it's what the band means that created the moment. Let me ask you – how'd you feel when I thanked you for Cor Unum?"

"I felt great."

"Indeed," said Marcus. "Did it make you feel like helping in other ways too?"

"Yes," replied Sam. "I just thought of another game-changing idea to share."

"Both answers," nodded Marcus, "weren't because of the band . . . they were because the band's your reminder of how it feels to be *recognized*. The band recognizes players for achieving something I wanted. To build the culture I want, I must *recognize recognition*."

"Just like Coach Knight said."

"Pfff," exhaled Marcus. "No one's in his league when it comes to dropping knowledge bombs."

"I know!" Sam smiled. "I get writer's cramp when he's around."

Marcus asked, "Want to really help this team in other ways?"

"Yes."

"Then what do you think of these?" said Marcus, turning his desktop screen.

"What are those?"

"Those," replied Marcus, "are another form of recognition for our culture. They're mock-ups of *helmet stickers*."

"Helmet stickers?" asked Sam. "What's that?"

"You really aren't a football fan. Helmet stickers are what they sound like – stickers for a football helmet. Just like the rubber in the band, the sticker's power is not in the adhesive . . . it's in the recognition."

"How do you earn a sticker?" asked Sam.

"Helmet stickers are traditionally given out for good plays on the field. But I want to do something different. The bands taught me a valuable lesson – there are 105 players on this team, but many will never get into a game. So, if helmet stickers are only for on-field performances, most players won't earn one. That could hurt morale more than help it. Because I want my players to live up to our values, I'll recognize them when they do. So I'll be recognizing great plays both on and off the field."

"Great idea, Coach," said Sam. "I've done a lot of logo design and found 'simpler' works better. That's why I like this design the most," he said pointing to the blue heart with a gold number 1 inside.

"You could be right," said Marcus.

"But can I make one suggestion?"

"Sure," replied Marcus.

"The only thing I'd add would be five horizontal lines on the right side of the number 1 . . . like this," said Sam as he drew a sketch. "Those five lines represent the five values of Cor Unum."

Marcus looked at the drawing and exclaimed, "You've done it again!'

Sam sat back and smiled. "I told you I designed logos."

"This is great!" said Marcus. "I'll send your idea to the designer and get these made."

"Glad to help, Coach."

"Me too," replied Marcus. "These could be even bigger than the bands since helmet stickers will be a new part of our culture."

"How so?"

"Helmet stickers have never been used here," explained Marcus, "so these stickers will create media attention. You might see your design everywhere."

"Wow," replied Sam. "Would it be good attention?"

"You have no idea," answered Marcus. "Since recruiting is so competitive, schools need something like this to separate themselves. If we do get some wins this year and some publicity, it could help beyond this season too."

"I've heard any publicity is good publicity."

"I wouldn't go that far," said Marcus. "These days players can do things schools don't want publicized. One of my biggest fears is a player doing something stupid, and making the program look bad. Recognition helps to prevent that."

"By keeping players doing what you want them doing?"

"Now you're getting it," smiled Marcus. "By recognizing players for what I want them doing on and off the field, I increase the chances those actions continue to happen. But a head coach can only see so much. That's why I have another idea for the helmet stickers."

"What's that?" asked Sam.

"Players can recommend teammates for stickers too. So instead of coaches watching and rewarding players, the entire team will do it. By being on the lookout for the things we want, the players spend less time doing the things we don't."

"I like it," said Sam. "You've figured this out. Coach Knight'd say you have 'selective detectives' working for you."

"I say he'd call it a conspiracy. I am also changing *how* the stickers are given out. The best way to impact the culture is by recognizing players in front of the team. So when I give out a sticker, I don't want it covert – I want a *celebration*. Do that right, and these stickers will bring out their best."

"Sounds like something Napoleon said," replied Sam.

"Napoleon?"

"Yes," smiled Sam. "A famous quote was, 'A soldier will fight long and hard for a bit of colored ribbon.'"

A smile crept across Marcus's mouth. "I'll have to remember that one. You're an interesting guy, Sam. Is there anything I can help with?""

"You did give me a band," said Sam pointing to his wrist.

"Come on."

"I've enjoyed getting together," Sam began. "And don't think I haven't learned anything. But there are two things you could help me with."

"Shoot," replied Marcus.

"My biggest problem's with a senior staff member. What makes it worse is he's my good friend. I go back and forth on letting him go. Have you had experience with firing people?"

"Experience!?" exclaimed Marcus, "Now that I'm head coach, it's my stock in trade. I've not only had to fire good people, I've also been on the other side of the firing table too. As for advice – firing someone's one of the toughest responsibilities for a leader. You'd have to be crazy to enjoy it. But letting someone go for the good of the team is a necessary evil of leadership. On the football field, your team won't win with too many turnovers. But, as a head coach, you learn that some turnovers are necessary to win. It's the same for business. Why might you fire him? What'd he do?"

Sam explained, "It's a combination of what he is and isn't doing. He's negative and the least supportive of the new culture. And I'm discovering he isn't producing like he leads us to believe."

"Roger. This is bothering you, huh?"

Sam nodded. "Keeping me up late is more like it."

"This might help," started Marcus. "After agonizing over firing someone, when I finally did it, not only did I feel better, but that person seemed relieved too. Here's something Coach told me: if you have to fire a person, that person has already fired himself."

"That does help. Coach got me so focused on my culture, I'm trying to be its crusader. Between his ideas and what you said, the writing's on the wall."

"You know he teaches with stories, right?" asked Marcus.

"Yes. His stories are enlightening."

"Well . . ." started Marcus, "I have one for you. As you know, there are 105 players on my team. Even though it's still football, one big difference between college and the pros is that instead of 105 players on the roster, a pro head coach must cut his team to 53. That's one of the toughest examples of firing there is."

"How so?"

"Imagine you're a pro football coach." replied Marcus. "You have 100 guys at preseason camp with similar talent level, and each wants to make the team. Now picture calling half of them into your office, and taking away their NFL dream and big money from their family."

"Ugh," grunted Sam, "that job doesn't sound so fun anymore."

"Affirmative. The grass is always greener. Now that you understand the job, here's the story. Before this coach became famous, he had to build his first winning team. In his first season, he experienced the pain of cutting half the team. The first round of cuts weren't difficult. Because some players weren't big or fast enough, he cut them. As training camp continued, he identified another group who didn't have great positional skills, and cut them too. He also removed a group who didn't understand his system. After whittling the team according to size, speed, and mental skill, he still had 10 players too many. With final cuts due, he hatched a plan. That next day, the coach placed 'Keep off the grass' signs around training camp. Since players were taking shortcuts on the grass instead of using the appropriate walkways, the coach wanted to see whether they would follow the signs. He sat in his office and watched. Most players followed the signs, but when the coach saw a player walking on the grass, he said, 'Cut that guy!' One of the assistant coaches asked for the coach's rationale and he replied, 'Cutting him is easy. If he can't follow my rules about walking on the grass, how's he going to follow my rules about playing on the field?'"

Marcus smiled and asked, "How'd I do? As good as Coach?"

"Not bad," smiled Sam. "But your delivery needs work."

"Aaahh. Hopefully you got the message."

"Loud and clear," replied Sam. "Now, I promise the other way to help won't take long, but this requires 100% compliance from the team. If you think I've helped you so far, this will blow your mind."

"What do you need?" asked Marcus.

"I need you to get every coach and player to answer 15 questions about themselves. They just go to a link, and it should take less than 15 minutes."

"What's it for?"

"It's a secret, so I need you to trust me," replied Sam. "I've shown you what I can do with logos. Let me show how my company can help the team."

"No funny business?" said Marcus.

"You have my word. And you'll see what we put together first. If you don't like it, don't use it. For confidence, Coach Knight knows the plan and he likes it."

"Okay," said Marcus. "If he's on board, I am too. Now show me the five lines on that helmet sticker one more time. . . ."

18

New Blood and Dead Wood

"Good morning," said Sam to the Stamina staff. "This is the first of four quarterly meetings this year, and I have lots to share. Since March is halfway over, I wanted to cover what Stamina's done this year and where we're going."

Sam motioned to the TV.

"I'll present the same material I presented to the board yesterday. But this meeting is different because it will end with us setting goals for quarter two. I want this meeting to prove that from now on, I'll be transparent. And the first thing I want to be transparent about is admitting I haven't been a great leader. But as I hope you've seen, I'm changing that."

Sam clicked to a baseball player on the first slide.

"A lot of the changes are due to Coach Knight's influence. He also helped me prepare this talk. Please bear with me because I can't tell a story like he does yet."

Sam looked at the slide.

"A young baseball player made it to the major leagues. He had natural talent, but his play was overshadowed by his bad behavior. Since he was playing well, he thought he could do whatever he wanted. If he struck out, he threw his bat and helmet. If he got called out, he screamed at the umpires. Once after failing on an important at-bat, he smashed the dugout water cooler and splashed water on his teammates. He was out of control and his teammates avoided him. Because of his good numbers, the team was afraid to reprimand him."

Sam paused.

"But one veteran player couldn't take it. He asked a videographer to produce a compilation of the player's wild behaviors. Once he had the video, the veteran cornered the young player and made him watch it. Although the young player was angered for being called out, he was embarrassed by what he saw. The veteran said, 'Look kid, I've been in this league a long time and guys like you never last. You have a choice to act foolish, but what you're doing will never be okay here. *That's not how we do things.*"

Sam clicked the next slide with an image of money.

"I want to apologize. And not for the way I told that story. I want to apologize, because I've been serving the wrong king. Maybe you've heard, 'cash is king.' And yes, money is important to our business. Because of the way we celebrated the two big capital raises, I might've given you the wrong impression about what's most important at Stamina. I've recognized there's a more important king to serve for Stamina to succeed. And that king," said Sam, clicking to a group photo from bowling night, "is *culture.*"

A few people clapped.

"Over the last four months, I've learned *culture is king*. And I unfortunately learned there's a difference between where our culture was and where I wanted it to be. I was disappointed to find our culture negative and uninspired. I was upset by the lack of collaboration and the gossip, but what upset me the most was realizing those problems were my fault."

Sam looked down.

"Moving forward, I accept full responsibility for our culture. When I took that responsibility, I began our lunch meetings, and have benefited from everyone's honest feedback. But leadership isn't just creating a product and starting a company. Leadership is hard, and forces me to make tough decisions. Actually, it forced me to make the toughest decision of my business career." Sam said, clicking to a picture of Sam and Rick.

"Last week . . . I let one of my best friends go."

Sam continued, "Rick and I met in college, and he was the second person to work at Stamina. But as you all know, Rick didn't embrace the culture we wanted moving forward. And that's the reason for my apology. Even though I got your feedback and knew what I must do, I wavered for months. That inaction hurt our culture and your experience. For that I'm ashamed."

"I wish I had acted sooner," continued Sam, "but I didn't. Rick and I met last week and he agreed to step away. He knows I'm talking to you today and we will remain friends. Moving forward, I'll no longer let anyone hold Stamina hostage based on time served, productivity, or a personal relationship."

"With that in the open, I don't want us worrying about the past. Stamina's a futuristic company, so let's keep our eyes on the future. But before we do," Sam said, clicking to a hotel drawing, "my second story takes us back to the 1880s."

"On a cold and rainy night in Philadelphia, a receptionist found himself working late. Around midnight, an older couple arrived, underdressed for the winter weather. The couple inquired about a room, but the receptionist reported the hotel was completely booked. Because he couldn't bear to turn them away, he offered for them to stay in his hotel room for the night. He said although it wasn't the penthouse suite, they'd be comfortable. The couple was hesitant, but accepted the room. When the older man checked out the next morning, he thanked the receptionist and said, 'You're the perfect person to run a hotel. Maybe I'll build one for you.'"

Sam paused.

"A few years later, that same receptionist was working at that same hotel when a letter arrived. With the letter was a train ticket to New York and an explanation. That older man was William Waldorf Astor and the ticket was an invitation to see the hotel he had built for the receptionist to manage. Ever heard of it? It was the Waldorf Astoria."

Sam briefly paused again.

"I've that learned people are the most important part of culture. My first story was about what happens to culture when the wrong person's on board. That second was about rewarding the right person when good deeds are discovered. That's why I need Dana to please come up front."

Dana cautiously stood up and walked up to the front.

"A few months ago, Dana visited my office and scared me."

Dana blushed.

"And it wasn't her tears that scared me. It was what they forced me to face – that Stamina wouldn't be successful without her. That day," said Sam, looking at the group, "Dana resigned. And not because she no longer liked Stamina, but because she *loved* it."

"Dana," Sam said, "you're the heart and soul of this place and the link to our 12th man. Because of your tireless effort, your positive attitude, and your honesty with me when I needed it, you've been selected for the first-ever Stamina 'Hard Charger' award!"

Sam pulled out a glass award shaped like Stamina's lightning-bolt logo. The entire staff cheered. Dana was overwhelmed, gave Sam a hug, and said, "Thank you."

As Dana sat down, Sam said, "The Hard Charger will be a quarterly award given to the staff member who best exhibits and upholds our core values. I'll explain with my final story."

Sam clicked to a picture of a crest.

"There was an inner-city high school having problems. Test scores and graduation rates were low. The only things this school ranked highly in were delinquency and expulsions. The school board hired consultants, and those consultants developed the core values for the school and incorporated them into a school crest. The plan was to place that crest in every room of the school as a reminder of those values. So when students went to class, to the gym, ate lunch, or even used the bathroom, they would see the crest. Years later, one of those consultants was teaching at a university. He discovered two students in his class had attended that high school. Excited to see how his crest had worked, he asked the students how many values they could remember. To his dismay, after four years in that school, they couldn't remember any! That professor learned a culture lesson: missions and values don't work from the top down; they work from the bottom up. Everyone must help create them because they don't work when they're in your face; *they work when they're in your heart*."

Sam clicked to a photo of Earth with the motto "Changing the way the world communicates" below it.

"Stamina began with a few software programs trying to change how sales were taught. As we grew, we realized our programs could also help HR departments train their teams. That's where the mission statement 'Powering the people who power businesses' originated. This mission wasn't incorrect then, but now it's incomplete. Yes, we power businesses, but that happens by improving *communication*. Stamina isn't a training company, it's a communication company! Like email and social media changed how people communicate, Stamina's games take communication to another level. Our games teach, and result in greater retention than other forms of learning. So, when someone asks you what Stamina does, now you have the bigger answer: we're changing the world, by changing the way the world communicates."

Sam paused.

"Along with the new mission, I want to explain our new values. The board and I didn't come up with these. These values came from the one-on-one conversations I've had with you. So be confident that Stamina's values are your values. Like the baseball story, these values will be how we do things here. And if we carry them out, we'll also carry out the mission."

Sam clicked to a new Stamina's logo with the quote "Our Games Make Information Stick."

"What makes learning from games better than traditional manuals is that information becomes more 'sticky.' Because I want our four values to be stickier, I made them into stickers." Sam pulled out a stack and handed out it to the group.

"To be a 'Hard Charger,' there are four values on that sticker you need to follow. The first is *Work Hard.* That's not just the hours you're here, but also the effort put into those hours. I'd rather you log five hours of hard work than ten just being in the building. At Stamina, we work on the hard things. This job isn't easy and neither's defending what we do. Games are a new form of learning, so we have to work harder than anyone."

"Number two is *Play Hard,*" Sam continued. "All work and no play doesn't just make you dull; it makes a dull culture. I value hard work, but you should also enjoy your work. Playing hard's about playing together. To demonstrate this value, you must get along with each other. You need to collaborate. Cooperate. And if there's conflict, and there should be, have strong opinions, but keep them weakly held."

Sam stuck a sticker on his laptop.

"Number three's *Be Curious*. Our business is ideas. We're going to need new ones to thrive. New ideas come from your curiosity. You should be on a relentless hunt for ways to make Stamina better. I want to be clear – there are no bad ideas here; the only bad idea is not being curious."

Sam paused.

"The fourth value is *Be Nice*. I shouldn't have to tell you, but, just in case, there should be no gossip, no resentment, and most importantly, no jerks allowed. I want open and honest communication. Talk *to* the person, not *about* them, and if we agree to disagree, be nice about it. Be a good person or you won't last here. And being nice isn't only being nice to our team or 12th man. This counts for your home life too."

Sam scanned the room.

"To summarize, the nice and curious person who works and plays hard is a Hard Charger. If you're a Hard Charger, you'll be recognized. And I want you to recognize each other. So, Shelly, please come up to the front."

Shelly stood to some applause and walked up with a big smile.

"Now Shelly, do you think you're up here for your bowling skills?"

"I doubt it," laughed Shelly.

"No," agreed Sam, "you're up here because of the energy you demonstrated on your walk up. I want to thank you for your enthusiasm, and recognize you for something you created at Stamina."

Shelly looked at Sam, confused.

"You might think," Sam continued, "ever since the bowling league, there are more high fives at Stamina. But recently, I realized that's not true. There haven't been any high fives at all."

Sam paused.

"The other day, when I showed Melissa these stickers, she said, 'High five,' and I gave her a one-handed version. That's when she corrected me and said, 'Come on, give me a high five like Shelly does!'"

Shelly bent over laughing.

"That taught me, we don't give high fives at Stamina." Sam continued. "We give *high tens*!'"

Sam raised both hands and Shelly gave him a high ten as the group cheered.

"Stamina doesn't give high fives." Sam repeated. "Those are cheap. We do hard work, we play hard, and we give high tens. And after lunch today, I hope to see a lot of them at our first-ever hack-a-thon."

Sam explained, "For the rest of the hour until lunch, we're setting quarter two goals. Then we'll have pizza, and begin a four-hour hack-a-thon. Here's how it works. I'm going to split you up into five teams of five people. Each team will have two engineers, and a member from customer service, sales, and marketing. Each team has to develop a new idea and present it at the end of the hack. As a group, we'll vote on the best idea."

The staff was pumped up.

"Don't thank me for this," continued Sam. "This idea was sparked by the project Raj and I are working on for the university, so thank him."

Raj stood up and took a bow.

"Finally, charging through this hack-a-thon, you'll be inspired by the sounds of our own DJ Ben on the wheels of steel."

There was more cheering.

"If you're not aware," continued Sam, "aside from customer service, Ben moonlights as a DJ. I found that out at our lunch together, and today he's going to use some fresh beats to give us some fresh ideas."

After Stamina set their goals for quarter two, they enjoyed the delicious pizza and Ben's music rocked the hack. The winning idea came from an intern, reminding Sam that a company needs "new blood" after removing "dead wood."

19

Changing the Game

"Come in guys. . . . Hey, nice sweatshirt," said Marcus to Sam.

"Thanks," said Sam. "Since I was dropping by, I wanted to rep the team."

"Don't leave out my jacket," said Brian pointing at his coat.

"Don't worry, Coach," smiled Marcus, "no one's forgetting you. I'm just planning my first spring game and it's been crazy."

"What's the spring game?" asked Sam.

"After signing day, the spring game's the biggest media event of the year. The game showcases the players we've got for the upcoming season. But what people don't see are the spring practices leading up to the game. We only got fifteen of them and they didn't go as I'd hoped."

"What Marcus is saying," Brian started, "is that the spring game is like a dress rehearsal for the season ahead. As a coach, I never liked the game. It's a lot about fan engagement, but having had a few players get injured, it wasn't worth it."

"Agreed," said Marcus. "But it's a chance for the players to see what game day is like. So I value the preparation more than the competition. The team will perform the walk to the stadium and warmup exactly like they will in September. That way we're not doing it for the first time when it counts."

"*Preparation is the separation*," smiled Brian. "So how'd the practices go?"

"Overall, the position coaches used the practices to teach the offensive and defensive schemes we'll be using. The guys are stronger and faster from winter training. Gunny's been amazing, but that's not a surprise. The surprise was a couple of guys transferring out. That gave our culture a little hit. I wish there was a better way to teach culture."

Brian looked at Sam and they smiled. Marcus said, "Alright you two. You're thick as thieves. What's up?"

Brian said, "That's why we're here today, Marcus. Sam has a solution to your 'communication' problem.'" Brian told Sam, "Come on, kid . . . show him."

Sam pulled out his phone. "Okay, do you remember that link you sent to the players?"

"Yes," answered Marcus. "I was wondering what happened with that."

"Sorry for the delay, but my engineers are big fans and they wanted it to look great the first time you saw it," he said, clicking an app icon that resembled the team's helmet sticker. "Coach, we're calling this your 'Cor Unum' game."

The app opened to display the words "Cor Unum" with the university's helmet underneath.

"Looks cool," said Marcus. "What is it?"

"This," answered Sam, "is what Stamina does. We take information you want to communicate and make it a game. As a game, there's a better chance of learning and remembering that information."

"What does it do?"

"Well . . ." replied Sam, "Coach thought instead of telling you how it worked, he wanted you to be the first one to play."

"Sure," said Marcus taking Sam's phone. "What do I do?"

"Hit the 'kickoff' button and answer the questions that follow. You'll be given 15 of the 1,800 questions contained on the game."

"1,800?"

"You bet," smiled Sam. "The players and the coaches answered 15 questions for us. 120 people times 15 is 1,800."

"Wow," replied Marcus. "Just hit this button and go?"

"Yup," said Sam, "and you only get 25 seconds per question. Just like a football play-clock."

"Ha!" said Marcus. "Here we go . . ."

Marcus hit the button and after the opening whistle, Marcus answered questions about hometowns, favorite songs, foods, and teams. When he completed the game, his score appeared on a leaderboard. Since he was the only player, his name was at the top.

"There!" said Marcus. "Number one! That was cool. Was the football moving forward and back when I was answering?"

"Yes," replied Sam. "Four correct answers in a row is a first down, and three first downs in a row is a touchdown."

"I didn't get one of those?"

"No, Coach," replied Sam. "You only got two questions right."

"Someone needs to know his team better," smiled Brian.

"You're right, Coach," replied Marcus. "Do I get to play again?"

"You don't just *get* to play again," answered Sam. "The key *is* to play again! The more you play, the more questions you get. The more questions you get right, the more points for the leaderboard. Each week, we'll declare new winners, but the purpose of playing is to get the team to learn about each other."

"This could be great," said Marcus.

"It's better," said Brian. "Don't you see what you've got? It's a *cultural accelerator*. And Sam, you can add new information too, right?"

"Yes," said Sam. "We can add anything you want to teach. So while they're building their biceps in the weight room, they can be building the culture here. Whether it's offensive or defensive ideas or your message of the week, it's another way to connect."

"This is amazing," said Marcus.

"And look at this, Coach," said Sam. "I used your helmet sticker idea too. The better a player does, the more helmet stickers he adds to his helmet. And if you look here . . . players can high five each other for good performances too."

"Maaan," said Marcus. "You were right about this guy, Coach. Should we use this?"

"It's more new ham,'" winked Brian. "And an important lesson about culture too. The game's secret isn't the information – it's the *repetition* of the information that makes it stick. Culture's like that too. Culture, just like national championships, doesn't happen by accident. It happens with *repetition of a consistent message*."

"I hear you, Coach," said Marcus. "With repetition, Cor Unum's gotten even more popular. Once everyone earned their band, a few players took things to another level."

"What happened?" asked Sam.

"A couple of the seniors got 'Cor Unum' tattoos." answered Marcus.

"What?" asked Sam. "For real? I'm not sure if that's cool or crazy."

"Although tattoos are more common these days," said Marcus, "it still takes a powerful idea to tattoo it on themselves. Those tattoos will be their reminder of this team someday."

"Wow," replied Sam. "I never had an idea someone tattooed on themselves before."

"When I was coaching," said Brian, "tattoos were rare. But when a player explained their tattoo, they always mentioned how important the idea was to them. Tattoos are a great form of marketing."

"Marketing?" asked Sam.

"Sure," replied Brian. "Marketing's about consistent messaging. A tattoo remains as a reminder for that person why they got it. The wristbands do that too, but they're way less permanent. You can take a band off easily, but a tattoo's more painful."

"So you're saying," replied Sam, "that a tattoo's an idea someone is marketing?"

"Yes, and you can apply that marketing idea to your cultures. Your goal's not to get your people to follow the culture for a week – you want them to follow for the long term. To do that, you must tattoo your message on their minds with consistent reps. That's how marketing works. So, in addition to being crusaders for your culture, think of yourselves as its marketers too."

"I can add to that," said Sam. "My team says marketing only works with consistent *follow-up*. If culture works like marketing, you can't say something once. You must keep following up until you get the result you want."

"That's right," said Brian. "If you remember – your Beliefs define culture. Your Behaviors reinforce it, and your Beings carry it out. So . . . if your Beings become the messages they hear the most, then culture requires consistent repetition of the messages you most want them to hear."

"Knew you'd find a lesson somewhere, Coach," said Marcus.

"Be grateful. And be grateful for what Sam put together for you too. His game is a cultural way to meet your players where they are. It presents your messages using media they use the most. Just like tattoos, technology like Sam's is more common now. As you get older, technology can pass you by. That can make you and your message irrelevant because no one can hear you anymore. Look at my phone – it works but it's outdated. And if I need to fix my computer, I call my grandkids. I never thought I'd fall behind, but I did. It's okay for me, but it's too early for you, Marcus. These players today are always on their phones. If you aren't using phones to connect with them, you're missing where they are. Instead of printed playbooks, you can teach in a way they like. *Good coaches know the playbook. Great coaches know their players.*"

"So should I try it out?" asked Marcus, smiling.

"You already tried it out," Brian told him. "I'm saying don't *leave it in the case.*"

"Okay," said Sam. "What does that mean?"

"You wanna tell him or should I?" Brian asked Marcus.

"You take it, Coach," smiled Marcus. "You tell it better anyway."

Brian looked at Sam.

"In the 1800s, there was a musician named Niccolo Paganini, who was known as the greatest violinist of his time. One legend claimed his skill came from a deal with the devil. Regardless how he got his ability, his compositions were inspiration for generations to come. Over his career, Paganini came into possession of many valuable violins. One of these was his favorite. As his health declined, Paganini sold, gave away, and donated those violins until only his favorite remained. In the final days of his life, he offered this violin to his birth city of Genoa, Italy, on one condition – that no one ever play that violin again. The city accepted and the violin was placed in its case. After 150 years of keeping this promise, in honor of the 150th anniversary of Paganini's death, Genoa decided to open the case and display this piece of music history. TV crews were there to capture the opening. But to everyone's horror, this priceless instrument was destroyed! The years in the case had rotted the wood. The world learned what's true about boats and airplanes. They seem safer while stationary, but that's not why they were built. Just like Paganini's violin, a boat or plane will decay faster with inactivity than on the high seas or higher skies. The moral is this: when you have a golden opportunity, *never leave it in the case.*"

Brian asked, "How was that?"

"Bravo," said Marcus as Sam nodded. "One of your best, maestro."

"Grazie. And my long-winded answer about this game. You shouldn't worry what will happen if you play. You should worry what'll happen if you don't."

20

Date Night

"Will people think we're weird?" asked Melissa across the restaurant table.

"Weird we're eating at an Indian restaurant?" asked Sam.

"No silly. Weird because we're going on another cruise. Are we 'cruisers' now?"

"Cruisers?" asked Sam.

"Yes," said Melissa. "Remember those couples we met who take cruises every year? This will be our second one in six months."

"If that's the definition, I guess we are," smiled Sam. "Didn't you have fun last time?"

"Sure! I hope we aren't taking the easy way out, not figuring out something else to do."

"Nah," said Sam. "It's a different boat and theme. I'm looking forward to seeing new islands too. I enjoyed all the cool stuff we did last time."

"You're right," said Melissa. "I'm already getting uptight about getting hit with work while we're on the boat. I need to get better at letting work go."

"I wish I had secret for that. But work follows me too. Just not like you."

"Not since you met your little 'culture coach,'" sneered Melissa.

"Wow," chuckled Sam. "Sounds like someone's jealous. Brian's helped me out and I enjoy his company. He's the teacher I always wish I had."

"I know," smiled Melissa. "I'm happy you're finally having a 'bromance.'"

"Bromance? He's too old for me, and he calls it 'mentor-tainment.'"

"Ooh," said Melissa. "I like that. Seriously, I'm glad you're helping each other."

"He's helping me way more than I'm helping him."

"Don't be too sure," said Melissa. "From what you've told me, he probably gets lonely."

Sam just nodded and asked, "Any more thoughts about the firm?"

"Well," replied Melissa, "this upcoming trip's reminding me it's hard to escape work. I wish they'd respect my vacation, but that's not how our firm works. And the more I move up, the more emails I get. I hope they leave me alone for a few days, but I doubt it."

"I want you to enjoy this next trip, Meliss."

"I just want to relax," Melissa said. "The biggest thing bothering me since the last trip has been my desire to change. I think that knot in my stomach isn't because I don't want to be a lawyer – it's because I want to be a lawyer *somewhere else*."

Sam listened.

"Ever since I became a lawyer, I've gotten emails from recruiters, but I never entertained them. Actually I took pride in acting uninterested, as if I had the best job. After we went on the first cruise, I started to respond to those emails. There are opportunities, but change is scary. I know it isn't career or life threatening, but I'm afraid to take action. But . . . I'm entertaining some ideas."

"That's a step," said Sam. "Any ideas you like?"

"Yes, but you might think it's weird."

"Weirder than being a 'cruiser?'"

"Not that weird," laughed Melissa. "I reached out to a pro bono coordinator. I wanted to see what was available. I was amazed how many people could use my help, but can't afford it. Pro bono work's required by our firm, but we're only allowed to take a few cases because it isn't billable. Seems like window dressing versus altruism."

"That's not weird," said Sam. "It makes you more amazing. Like a super-lawyer."

"Yeah, like Erin Brockovich, right?"

"Call it what you want," replied Sam, "but you're on to something. Any areas where you'd like to help?"

"I have ideas, but one thing's clear; the pro bono work I've done left me feeling good. I want more work that feeds my soul."

"Well," started Sam, "I don't know about feeding your soul, but I've got an idea for you."

"Oh yeah?"

"Yes," replied Sam. "I wanted to cover it on the cruise, but 'date night' can work."

"What is it?"

"Well," Sam explained, "you know how you've helped me with the Stamina employee and sales contracts?"

"Yes," said Melissa, "and I don't know if I'd call it help. I remember completely writing them when you got started."

"Tomato, tohmahto. Now that I'm taking a deeper look at Stamina, I realize how much legal work's involved. As the company's grown, so has our need for lawyers . . . and our spending."

"This isn't what I meant by 'pro bono,'" joked Melissa.

"Ha! That's not what I'm saying. What if you came on board at Stamina? We have enough work to keep you busy and it'd be fun to work together."

"I don't know," said Melissa. "I've seen relationships get stressed when couples work together. . . ."

"Come on. More stressed than we are now?"

"You've got a point. What would my position be? House lawyer?"

"More like 'house mother,'" smiled Sam. "You know that's what the team calls you anyway."

"What?"

"Yeah," said Sam, "it's a good thing. You being at the bowling nights and decorating at the office showed that you're the 'mother hen' of Stamina. I want to make the position official."

"Hmmm, could be interesting. You know lawyers at my level don't come cheap."

"I had a feeling," smiled Sam. "So what do you think? One of my biggest regrets is you haven't been a big part of Stamina."

"Well, after spending more time around you and the team lately, I see I could shape up the place."

"Ha!" laughed Sam. "Already taking over and I didn't even hire you yet! We can discuss this further on the cruise, but I didn't want to wait. When you told me having children could limit your career, it affected me. I know we haven't talked about it, but I do want kids. We've been so busy, the topic never comes up. We're getting older and I want to protect the health of our baby."

"Whoa," said Melissa with a smile. "You really have been thinking about this stuff, haven't you? Our baby? Should I get a pregnancy test?

"I mean our future baby. Yes, I've been thinking about it, and if having kids would stop your career, it won't at Stamina. Since we're in our 30s, I want us to be smart and safe about starting a family. No pressure, but your biological clock is ticking. . . ."

"Oh my god," laughed Melissa. "No pressure? You just talked about changing my job, having kids, and getting old! You might want to read a book on tact. But I'm glad you brought those up, Sammy. These have been in the back of my mind too. You're getting me excited, so you'd better be serious."

"Dead serious, babe. It's a win-win. You get less stress, and use your talents how you want. I get to be around you more and we build Stamina together. And it gives our family the possibility to grow if we choose. And what we choose is most important – not your firm, not your mom, or my parents either."

"We have a lot to cover on the boat." Melissa smiled. "Isn't that what 'cruisers' do?"

21

Cherish or Perish

"Global headquarters?" asked Brian pointing to the words at the front entrance.

"Geez!" replied Sam, "You see everything. At least pretend to miss things so I can point out my progress, okay?"

"Ha! Okay, give me the tour."

As Brian entered Stamina, he felt a new energy. He saw staff members working together as Sam showed off the cosmetic updates to the four huddle rooms. Sam proudly explained how each one had a wall dedicated to one of Stamina's core values.

"Another cool thing," said Sam, "is that the staff refers to each of these rooms as either the 'Work,' 'Play,' 'Curious,' or "Nice' room."

"Great form of repetition for your values. And what's that?" Brian asked, pointing to a digital clock.

"Oh, that's our countdown clock. Since we set the quarterly goals, the engineers bought the clock to remind everyone that time's always ticking. It also tracks the time until our next hack-a-thon. Since quarter four's huge in the tech space, it's my reminder to be ready for that."

"No matter how you use it," said Brian, "it's another great idea. Like the motivational messages I see here too. They promote good energy."

"You want energy?" replied Sam, "Let's go see the engineers."

Sam led Brian to the engineering room.

"Hey Raj!" called Sam. "Look who's here!"

When Raj saw Brian, he jogged over.

"Hey, Coach!" said Raj. "What's the word?"

"The word is your game's a big hit at the university. Coach Chase told me the players are addicted."

"Yes!" Raj raised his hands and said, "High ten, Coach!"

Brian slapped his hands.

"So that's the 'high ten' I've heard about?" asked Brian.

"The one and only," smiled Sam. "It's getting addictive, too."

Brian said, "Thanks for the work you put into the game, Raj. As the former coach, I want to see the team succeed, and even more so because Coach Chase is my former player. Sam's shared how hard you've worked, and I wanted you to know you're appreciated."

"Thanks, Coach," replied Raj. "I'm happy to help, and Coach Chase sent new information to keep the game changing. But don't think this costs me time. Sam and I are using the same concept here and we're going to make versions for other companies too. So what started as a passion has become a new product for Stamina to change how companies communicate."

Sam gave Raj a high ten.

"Nice. You're on to something. If it helped us, it could help every team. Just do me a favor . . ." Brian said as he put his arm around Raj, "wait until after the season to give it to the competition, okay?"

"Sure thing, Coach!"

On their tour, Sam continued pointing out little changes around Stamina. They ended up in Sam's office and assumed their usual positions.

"I'm proud of you, Sam. You've turned this ship around and are headed in a positive direction."

"This Zodiac's moving," Sam replied, "and we've got good people on board. I'm having a great time leading, and feel like when I started the company. And by empowering my people, they're coming up with great ideas too.

It's made my work easier and has given Melissa and me more time. I followed your prescription and we have another cruise coming up."

"Just another perk of 'leveling up' as a leader." Brian smiled.

"Leveling up?" asked Sam, opening his golden notebook.

"Yes. When we met, if I drew an organizational chart of Stamina, it would've looked horizontal and your name would've been everywhere. But as you defined Stamina's divisions and the leadership roles of the people who led them, you made the chart vertical and leveled up to the top. That's where you should sit."

"You're right." replied Sam. "I was too involved with coding and sales scripts. Heck, I was changing the coffee in the cantina! Now team leaders report to me, and I have meetings to cover plans. My day's easier, my people are better, and Stamina's more efficient than ever."

"Welcome to the *culture chain*," replied Brian. "Just like your 'org' chart should be vertical, that's how your culture should look too. They should have the same flow."

"Flow?"

"Yes," replied Brian. "I've explained the culture of a business as its life force. That life force should flow in certain directions. For instance, when delivering your culture's mission, vision, and values, those should flow *down* the chain because a leader's role is to deliver those to your people. But regarding problems of a culture, those should flow *up* the chain. Unfortunately, many companies experience the reverse. A few months ago, that was happening at Stamina! Unwanted culture flowed from the bottom up, and you were sharing problems from the top down."

"Hard to believe."

"Be glad you're driving a Zodiac," Brian grinned, "and not an aircraft carrier."

"True," said Sam. "Leveling up has required *delegating*. It was hard to do at first, but I'm improving. And the more I delegate, the better my people get! Did I tell you about Dana?"

"No," replied Brian. "What's going on?"

"Like you said, Dana is Stamina's star. A couple weeks ago, she had an idea. Since the customer service, sales, and marketing divisions were working more closely, she wondered if we could combine the divisions. We tinkered with the idea, and created the 'Customer Success' division of Stamina. We'll still have three teams devoted to service, sales, and marketing, but now they're under one umbrella. And naturally, I named Dana the head of Customer Success."

"Great moves," smiled Brian.

"And each of the three teams has a team leader! So Dana and three others leveled up?"

"Ta-da!" smiled Brian. "That's why your stress is down and productivity's up. By adding more links in the vertical chain between you and the staff members, you get to focus more on leading than on the day-to-day operations."

"And we aren't finished yet."

"Nope," smiled Brian. "Business development is never finished. A culture's either growing or dying. That's why – now that your culture's improving – you must understand the *Law of Cherish or Perish*."

"Sounds like another lesson," said Sam, grabbing his pen.

"Right! The law is simple to understand – what your culture cherishes will survive, and what it ignores will wither and die. But if I summed up the law with one word, it would be 'attention.' Have you heard of the Hawthorne effect?"

"No," replied Sam. "What's that?"

"That's about the power of shining the light of attention. In the 1920s, a Chicago factory called the Hawthorne Works studied whether workers were more productive in higher or lower levels of light. When the researchers turned up the lights, the workers', productivity increased. But when they dimmed the lights, productivity increased again! Only when the study ended did performance decrease. Interpretations suggest the increases in productivity happened because researchers *paid attention to the workers*! This power of attention has been dubbed the Hawthorne effect."

"That's interesting," said Sam. "But what's the point?"

"The point is that productivity increased whether they raised or dimmed the lights. It wasn't the light, but the focus on the workers that made them more productive. So the best way to 'illuminate' someone is to pay attention to them! And the best time to cherish your Beings is when they're exhibiting Behaviors that match your Beliefs. When you turn the lights of attention on someone or something in your culture, it becomes more visible. A leader must learn to correctly shine the lights."

"Is this about recognition?" asked Sam.

"Recognition is part of the law, but I'm talking about something bigger, called *Cultivation*."

"Cultivation?" asked Sam.

"Yes," replied Brian. "Ever have a garden at home?"

"My mom used to grow strawberries."

"Okay," said Brian. "Think about her garden. To grow healthy fruit, your mom needed to give those fruits the right attention and cherish what stimulated growth. To produce those strawberries, she needed good dirt, water, and fertilizer, right?"

"Yes."

"Well," replied Brian, "your culture's like that garden. The Law of Cherish or Perish demands attention to the cultural stimulators that make things grow."

"Cultural stimulators?" asked Sam.

"Yes," replied Brian. "To simplify, I'll categorize them into six areas. And the great news is you're already using them. That's why your culture's improving.

Sam nodded and took notes.

"As you learned, the first powerful way to stimulate culture is with *Recognition*. This can be an award or publicly recognizing someone's performance. The second stimulator is closely related – *Appreciation*. They're grouped differently because Recognition's for something a person *did*, while Appreciation's for *who they are*."

"Sounds complicated," said Sam.

"Not at all," replied Brian. "Both are forms of feedback, just about different things. Think about it like this. If you see someone *do something* you like, giving them a high ten is Recognizing. But if you see something *about someone* you like, like their courage or attitude, telling them is Appreciating. In both cases, you're *magnifying what you'd like to manifest* more of."

"I like that. Makes perfect sense. I do both sometimes, but I could be better."

"You're the gardener," smiled Brian, "and the cultivator of your culture."

Sam wrote that down.

"The next culture stimulator is one most businesses forget: *Training*."

"What kind of training?" asked Sam.

"Any kind your people need!" exclaimed Brian. "Most cultures act like injured athletes – they 'overcompete' and 'undertrain.' Many young athletes don't train enough because they're too busy competing, and businesses often falter because their people do the same – they get a week of training at the beginning of their career and have to figure out the rest. Roles, job descriptions, and technology are constantly changing. But training at most companies doesn't match that change."

"That's exactly what Stamina does!" exclaimed Sam. "We use games to help businesses train their people. And the hardest part of our business isn't developing the games; it's convincing failing companies they need them! Unfortunately, when a business begins to struggle, they cut costs – and training's the first to go."

"Training must always be fertilizing a business and its culture."

"You're preaching to the choir," smiled Sam. "What's next?"

"The next two go together like the first two. These are *Rituals* and *Symbols*. Rituals are the unique behaviors of your culture. According to the Law of Cherish or Perish, if those rituals don't happen often, they lose power. Remember that Haka video?"

"Of course."

"Imagine," continued Brian, "instead of at every game, the All Blacks only did the Haka once a year. Would it be a powerful culture stimulator?"

"Probably not."

"You're right," smiled Brian. "For rituals to become stimulators of culture, they must happen regularly. Take your high ten. Are people using them outside the bowling league?"

"Yes," said Sam, "Raj gave you one today."

"Right on! That kind of repetition doesn't only stimulate your culture; it made me want to be part of it. I also mentioned Symbols," continued Brian. "Rituals use human action to stimulate your culture; symbols are inanimate stimulators. A great example would be your logo or the core values painted in your huddle rooms. Those are symbols constantly stimulating the culture you want."

"Got you," said Sam. "Are the uniforms and stickers symbols too?"

"Sure! As long as they stimulate things you want."

"Roger," said Sam. "What's the final stimulator?"

"The final stimulator is one you're having success with: *Collaboration*. Not long ago, your people weren't working together. But after your meetings and social events, Stamina's power has multiplied. With collaboration, projects happen faster, and your people develop a support system. After seeing the energy today, collaboration is working here."

"Thanks," said Sam. "Each stimulator has positively influenced our culture."

"Cultivated," said Brian with a wink.

"Yes," laughed Sam, "cultivated. Like a garden, I have to keep fertilizing, right?"

"Just like your mother's strawberries. It's all about attention. Lack of attention kills a garden. And if you're confused about what to do, remember this universal life-truth: *What gets watered is what grows.*"

22

Brick by Brick

"Alright!" screamed Gunny over the music. "This is what we've been waiting for!"

The team was crowded in a semicircle around Gunny who stood on a bench by the squat rack. The barbell was filled with so many plates that it was bending. "For our final lift," yelled Gunny, "Thurston's going for the school's oldest lifting record!"

The players started cheering around the player about to make the attempt. To clear a path, they spread apart to give all 6-foot-6 and 310 pounds of Mitch Thurston room to approach the bar.

"In case you can't count," screamed Gunny, "there are seven plates on each side!"

The team went wild.

"And if you who can't add, the bar's loaded with 675 pounds!"

The players continued jumping up and down.

Mitch Thurston was ready. With a thunderous yell he walked through the gauntlet of teammates, and with Gunny moving behind him and two assistant coaches moving to each side of the bar, Thurston pulled under the bar and placed it on the back of his neck.

"This's for history, Mitch! Leave no doubt!" Gunny screamed as Thurston set his feet.

With another yell, Thurston bent the bar across his back, forcing it to leave its resting place. As Thurston took a step back with each foot, the team went silent. The only sounds were the music, an inhalation of air into Thurston's lungs, and Gunny screaming, "Let's gooooo!"

Thurston's body lowered. As he squatted, his descent slowed to a stop. When he reversed this motion, the team erupted. Thurston's ascent had Gunny unsure he'd complete the lift. The spotters stayed close as Thurston continued to rise.

"Get it! Get it!" encouraged Gunny.

After the all-out effort, Thurston returned to standing. As Thurston racked the bar, pandemonium ensued. Players were jumping and hugging and high fives were everywhere. They'd all just been part of history.

Gunny jumped onto the bench and yelled, "That, men, was the greatest lift I've ever been part of. Join me in congratulating the new all-time squat record holder, Mitch Thurston!"

The players celebrated again.

"Over this year, you've gotten to know me," Gunny began, "and my love of traveling. My favorite place is Italy. And not for the food, but because the Roman architecture inspires me. Rome's a great example of people leaving their mark. Arenas like the Colosseum still stand after thousands of years. Although its architects are gone, their mark lives on. Question: Didn't it feel amazing to leave your mark tonight?"

The players roared.

"That feeling gave me the inspiration for our final Cauldron before summer break."

Some players smiled like Gunny was kidding.

"You thought you were done?" asked Gunny. "Did you think it'd be that easy? I knew some of you, like Thurston, could leave their mark tonight, but I wanted to give everyone a chance. So before my final Cauldron, I have one question. . . . Who's ready to leave their mark?"

The team cheered.

"Good. Then Coach Chase will lead you out," Gunny said, pointing to Marcus.

"Alright, men," yelled Marcus. "I have a feeling tonight will be something you never forget. Follow me!"

Marcus marched out of the weight room, followed by the team. Marcus led them outside to the stadium entrance gate. A lone security guard held the gate open as the players walked through and huddled around Marcus.

"Okay, men!" shouted Marcus. "A lot of history has happened in this stadium. You know players and coaches who have left their mark. Some of you will get the chance to carve your name into our history this season, but tonight everyone will get that chance."

Marcus left the stadium and led the team down a brick path until he reached an area marked off with caution tape.

After the team assembled around him, he said, "If you go to this school, you know where we're standing! Most days of the year, this is a brick path helping students to get to class. But on a handful of Saturdays, this path becomes the roadway of our greatest tradition, the 'Player's Walk.' If you've walked this path on game day as thousands cheered you on, you understand its importance. Every player before you, great or small, has walked this same path – and this tradition will continue after you're gone."

Marcus continued, "The Player's Walk is a unique tradition because everyone covers the same journey. No one is special on the Player's Walk – you're all equally valuable. You're all players. I'm highlighting this tradition because this team still has one weakness – one that can break us apart. I hope Gunny's Cauldron will eliminate that weakness tonight."

"Before Gunny starts, I have a story explaining our weakness. Two proud lions," Marcus exclaimed, "approached a pool of water. Both of them were thirsty and one lion said, 'Step aside while I drink first.' The other lion roared, 'Back off! I'm drinking first.' Then they started fighting. They were so focused on their battle, they never noticed the vultures circling above. The vultures said to each other, 'Look at this! Lion! We're gonna eat lion! Tired and bloodied, the lions finally noticed the birds and realized their mistake and saw that the pool was big enough for both of them. They stopped fighting, laughed at their mistake, and drank together."

"Ego!" shouted Marcus. "*Ego is the killer of culture.* And tonight it ends. No more pointing fingers or worrying who deserves more attention or isn't appreciated. We're one team here. No one wins alone. Football's a team effort, and that's what Cor Unum's all about! You're starting to get it, but we're out of time. And tonight, Gunny has the solution."

Gunny moved inside the roped-off area and stood between two palettes of bricks. The bricks on one palette were blue and the others gold.

"As you see," yelled Gunny hopping on the stack of blue bricks, "we're doing some construction tonight! Our university has been kind enough to grant us the privilege of leaving our mark on this section of the Player's Walk. Tonight, you can earn the opportunity to lay the bricks this and future teams will tread over forever. That opportunity will be earned by passing my Cauldron. Is that clear?"

"Yes sir!" called the players.

"Good! I call this Cauldron 'The Weight of Bricks.' A standard brick, like the ones here, weighs just 4.5 pounds. After seeing what Mitch did with 675 pounds, that shouldn't sound like much. But I guarantee you'll never forget what a brick weighs. Now everyone get inside the tape, grab two bricks, and stand where the old bricks have been removed."

The players did as instructed.

Then Gunny yelled, "Okay, everyone, get in ten lines facing me."

The players quickly moved into position.

"The three rules of this Cauldron are simple. Rule number one: when I say to bring your bricks up, lift the bricks up. Lift them to the front, to the side – I don't care – but the bricks must reach shoulder height. Rule number two: when I say bring your bricks down, let them hang at your sides and relax. And rule number three: whatever you have to do, don't let your bricks down until I say. If you quit and lower your bricks, everyone fails. Is that clear?"

"Yes, sir!" yelled the team.

"Good! The coaches and I will make sure you're maintaining proper height. If we say you're getting low, do something about it. This will be tough and you'll experience pain. That being said . . . tell me," Gunny screamed, "which one of you's gonna give up first?"

There was silence.

"Excellent!" yelled Gunny. "Then let's try it. When I say up, lift your bricks up. Keep them there until I say down. When I say down, put them down. Got it!?"

"Yes sir!" chanted the team.

"Everybody . . . up!" screamed Gunny as he clicked his stopwatch. The players lifted their bricks. When his stopwatch read 25 seconds, Gunny instructed, "Everybody down!"

The players lowered their bricks.

"Nice job men! Congratulations! You made it 25 seconds with 4.5 pounds. Let's try a little more. . . . Ready . . . up!"

Gunny clocked 25 seconds and commanded, "Everybody down!"

A few players groaned after this rep, and Gunny attacked. "You kidding me? That was rep two and I'm already hearing weakness? Ready . . . up!"

And the players again lifted their bricks for 25 seconds. When they lowered them, the groans got louder.

"Come on, guys!" screamed Gunny. "No whining! Weakness is contagious. Get tough! Cor Unum right here! Everybody up!"

The team lifted and lowered their bricks for the fourth rep. Gunny repeated this procedure for reps five, six, seven, eight, and nine. During those, players began to struggle. Arms were shaking and instead of groaning, players yelled in agony. During repetitions 10, 11, and 12, players shifted to encouraging one another. On repetition 15, two players made a breakthrough.

Joe Wilson, the kicker and one of the smallest players, confided in Trevor Nelson, "I'm shot, Trev, I can't make it."

"You can do it!" replied Trevor. "Don't give up!"

Trevor instinctively lowered his arms under Joe's and helped keep Joe's bricks up.

"Everybody down!" screamed Gunny. "You still a team of individuals? You still got ego telling you to do it alone?"

"I don't have another one, Trev," whispered Joe.

"No. Joe, I've got an idea," said Trevor. "On the next lift, just place your bricks on my shoulders. It doesn't break the rules."

When Gunny ordered, "Everybody up!" for the 16th rep, Joe tried what Trevor suggested and Gunny ran over.

"Nice technique, Wilson," whispered Gunny. "But why let Nelson do all the work?"

Other players noticed Trevor helping and copied the technique on the 17th rep. Gunny then said to Trevor, "If you're a team player, why are you keeping it secret?"

After the 17th rep, when Gunny yelled, "Everybody down!" Trevor countered, "Yo! Everybody! When Gunny yells, 'Up' put your bricks on each other's shoulders. It doesn't break the rules and he's allowing it! Partner up and work together!"

Gunny smiled and yelled, "Everybody up!" one last time. He never clicked his stopwatch, knowing each player could effortlessly support the others for hours.

Gunny let that final rep go longer than the others to prove the point. Players were smiling even though their arms still burned. They'd passed the final Cauldron. When Gunny said, "Bricks down!" they cheered.

"Great work," began Gunny. "There are two things you should have learned during those 20 minutes. First, working together makes things easier, and second, the weight of little things can eventually become a lot – no matter how strong you are. Those 4.5-pound bricks are like other little things you carry around – like *negativity* and *complaints*. Tonight I wanted you to understand that if you carry ego around long enough, it can break you and this team down."

Gunny pointed to the bricks.

"These bricks represent the negative things holding this team back. Tonight, you drop them! We're going to symbolize dropping weakness by leaving those bricks on this path. Then, once they're in place, no team here will ever forget to leave the little things behind."

The team was silent.

Gunny looked at Marcus and said, "Coach, they passed my test. Give them their final instructions."

"What I liked about that Cauldron," began Marcus, "was some of you stepped up in crisis and showed quick thinking and leadership. How you leave your mark will demand both. The university has agreed to let us place these bricks down however we want. The design you choose should represent this team and honor the teams to come. Gunny and I aren't helping. Figure it out as a team. But when I leave for home tonight, I want to walk over something I will forever be proud of. Don't let us down."

And with that, Marcus and Gunny walked away.

With the head coaches gone, some senior leaders took charge, but no one could decide on the pattern. As time ran out, Max Marshall came through. Since he had experience laying brick with his father, the team listened, got a plan, and started construction.

Marcus was proud of his team. They were stronger and embracing his philosophy. The strength gains were evident in record-setting performances. The acceptance of his philosophy was confirmed when he saw his players' contribution to the Player's Walk. The bricks were arranged into a gold mosaic with a blue heart for its center. And under the heart, blue bricks spelled *Cor Unum*.

23

Summer Fun

"Welcome back," said Sam.

"Good to be back," replied Brian. "Nice tan you've got going."

"I do, don't I? Can't believe the summer's halfway over. You might not be as tan, but it looks like you've lost weight."

"Jawohl," smiled Brian patting his belly. "I'll take that compliment. I've started back at the gym, shaped up my diet and my waistline too. It feels good to get some muscle back."

"Good work," said Sam. "I'm not a workout warrior, but the softball league's gotten pretty serious."

"Softball? Isn't this a bowling company?"

"Well," started Sam, "the bowling league was such a success, the staff wanted to get outdoors for the summer. It's a coed slow-pitch league. We aren't the best, but thanks to Dana, we're the best dressed."

"Look good, feel good. Feel good, play good," said Brian.

"We've got the first part," smiled Sam. "We're working on the 'play good.'"

Brian scanned Stamina's office. "Your office looks great."

"Thanks," said Sam. "We've added more logos and . . . ohhh . . . we've got our new mantra!"

"Mantra?"

"Yes," replied Sam. "Since Cor Unum was a success for the team, I wanted a mantra for Stamina. After searching for weeks, leave it to Raj to come up with it again."

"What happened?" asked Brian.

"During my search, I read books and studied other companies. Then one day, having coffee in the cantina, Raj gave me a eureka moment."

"They're the best, right?" asked Brian. "What did Raj say?"

"Raj and another engineer were talking, and right before Raj gave him a high ten, he said, 'Bring it in!' Soon as I heard it, I realized those three words had different and important meanings at Stamina."

"And those are?" asked Brian.

"One is *togetherness*," replied Sam. "When a coach says, 'Bring it in,' that means for everyone to assemble. Because Stamina's meeting more often as a team, those words represent the power of us getting together."

"I like that," said Brian.

"Another is revenue. Stamina creates ideas to produce profit. So, to our Customer Success division, 'Bring it in' represents bringing in money with new sales."

"Nice," agreed Brian.

"The final way we use 'Bring it in' is giving recognition for a job well done. Like when we give a high ten. Adding those words to our high ten has made it our culture's strongest ritual."

"Perfect," smiled Brian. "You've got a winner."

"I know," agreed Sam. "If I didn't, I wouldn't have painted it across that back wall!"

"Yeah," chuckled Brian. "Guess not. I like how the mantra came from within because organic ideas stick best. Raj is another Stamina star, huh?"

"Yes. He's a great programmer, and an even bigger idea guy. Did you know he has degrees from MIT and Cal Tech?"

"No," said Brian, "sounds impressive."

"Not half as impressive as his stand-up comedy career," said Sam.

"Really?"

"Yes," replied Sam, "and he's got our highest bowling average too! But his best qualities are his humility and willingness to help everyone. That's why I created a new position for him."

"Leveling up?" smiled Brian.

"Yes. After Raj and I worked on the game, and watching him during our first two hack-a-thons, I realized he's better at designing than programming. And that's saying something. So I created a new position called 'Head of Product.' Now Raj's in charge of all programs, and another engineer moved up as chief technical officer. Two more people leveling up and Stamina gets better."

"And your job gets easier," Brian reminded him. "Your org chart is shaping up."

"Vertically and horizontally," smiled Sam. "Since we're on org charts, come meet our newest hire."

Sam and Brian entered the huddle room with the core value 'Nice' on the wall. Brian saw a woman doing paperwork.

"Meliss," said Sam, "meet the man you've heard so much about. This is Brian Knight."

Melissa jumped up from her chair and before he could extend his hand, Melissa gave him a hug.

"So nice to finally meet. Sam's told me so much, and I want thank you for everything you've done for Stamina . . . and us."

"Nice to meet you," smiled Brian. "As for helping, it's my pleasure. Sam's a great student."

Sam smiled.

"So why are you here today?" asked Brian.

Before Melissa could answer, Sam said, "She works here now!"

"Wow!" replied Brian. "Congratulations!"

"Don't congratulate us yet," smiled Melissa. "I'm just getting started, and seeing these incomplete documents, I'm having second thoughts."

"Ha!" laughed Sam. "Hard to find good help these days, right, Brian?"

Brian was wise and stayed quiet.

"Seriously," began Melissa, "there's a lot of work, but I'm enjoying it. I was scared to leave my law firm, but it's been like jumping from an airplane."

"How so?" asked Brian.

"Fear only exits before you jump. So you decide how long the fear lasts. Most people sit at the edge of the plane in fear and never jump. But those who jump start flying."

"Great analogy," said Brian. "What are you working on?"

"Mostly contracts," replied Melissa, "Stamina uses them with employees and companies. Everything from employee benefits to terms of business relationships. I'm the whole legal team, but Sam hasn't given me an official title since Director of Awesome isn't available."

"Too bad," laughed Brian. "Any ideas for what you'd like to do after this paperwork?"

"Actually, that's how Sam got me interested in making the move."

"That," interrupted Sam, "and working with your handsome husband, right?"

Melissa just paused stoically, smiled, and addressed Brian.

"I don't have the exact idea, but I'd like start a pro bono way for Stamina to help the community. I want to use my skills for the greater good. I enjoyed doing nonprofit work in the past, so it would be great to try that here."

"Smart and noble." Brian smiled and said to Sam, "And you're smart adding her to the team."

Brian said to Melissa, "I see you're busy. Will you join us for lunch? We could flesh out some non-profit ideas."

"Sounds great," Melissa replied with a smile.

"Perfect," said Brian. "Now excuse us, Sam and I have work to do. If I don't teach him something, he'll think he doesn't need me anymore."

"See you at lunch," said Melissa.

Brian sat in the Stamina cantina while Sam made them coffees.

"I'm so glad Melissa's here," Sam said. "It removed her stress, and we're acting more like a normal couple."

"Best move ever," replied Brian.

Sam nodded and handed Brian his coffee.

"Did we talk about this?" pointing to the papers taped on the refrigerator door.

"No," replied Brian. "What are those?"

"Those are new weekly items on what we're calling the Ventilator."

"The Ventilator?" asked Brian. "Who thought of that?"

"Take a guess." Sam prompted.

"Raj again?"

"Right!" said Sam. "Since the cantina's a 'high-traffic' area, everyone ends up here during the day. After the bowling league, some funny pictures started appearing on the fridge. I asked Raj if he thought the jokes were okay. Since he's an actual comedian, he said it was great – as long as it stayed in jest. He called it the Ventilator because it's a way to vent our stress with humor."

"That guy is smart," said Brian as he got up and examined the papers. "These are funny."

"Yeah, they really are. We let everyone know nothing malicious would be tolerated. We took a preemptive strike at the proverbial water cooler by making a place to spread laughter instead of gossip."

"It's great," agreed Brian. "Congratulations for taking your culture to the highest level."

"Really?" asked Sam. "By putting jokes on the fridge?"

"No, Sam. It's not about the jokes. It's the environment. Don't you see? Eight months ago, you had scared staff jockeying for position. But you've built a foundation of trust. That trust is the bedrock a culture stands upon. If there's no trust, a culture won't last. Now that you've established trust, your culture is thriving. Trust is the foundation of a great culture, but there's another layer and you have it here. That Ventilator says you have a culture of trust where people *enjoy* working together! Trust is so strong, they can safely tease each other. When a culture reaches that level, you have what other companies envy."

"What's that?" asked Sam.

"The 'F-word.'"

Sam looked confused.

Brian said, "Before I scare you, I'll explain. When you were born, you had one requirement: fun. As a kid you pursued fun and avoided anything unenjoyable. Even in high school your job was still to have fun. Then in college, the fun started to mix with responsibility. You spent the next four years having fun preparing for a career. So, up until about 22 years old, the world said fun was the primary directive."

"I used to think high school and college were tough," said Sam. "But they were fun times."

"Yes, and unfortunately," continued Brian, "when you graduated, the world considered you an adult. And as a responsible adult, you must replace fun with money. As you moved from job to job, your primary directive became making as much money as possible. Then you founded Stamina, and money replaced fun completely."

"That's my story."

"Nah," smiled Brian. "You're better off than most people. Most are convinced to spend 50 years making money and then have some fun. So, until 65 or 70 years old, the world says don't have fun since money's the primary directive."

"You've blown my mind again."

"Thanks," smiled Brian. "Recognize the F-word is *fun*. And having fun should be the responsibility of every adult. So be proud of yourself, Sam. You've created a rare company that's a worthwhile and fun place to work. When a culture's fun, people love their work. When people love their work, they don't leave. And fun isn't only good for retention, it's great for recruiting too. There are great people out there who love what they do, but hate where they work. Stamina's culture will attract them."

"Fun can do that?" asked Sam.

"You know Southwest Airlines?" asked Brian.

"Of course."

"What's your first thought about them?" asked Brian.

"Bags fly free?"

"Nice!" laughed Brian. "Well, their marketing's working. Southwest was started by a maverick named Herb Kelleher. Herb wanted to shake up the airline industry. He took on destinations other airlines wouldn't touch and proved airlines could be profitable. But his biggest lesson was about having fun."

"What'd he do?" asked Sam.

"For fun?" replied Brian. "Lots of things. He staged crazy promotional events, but I loved Southwest's 'brown shorts.'"

"Brown shorts?"

"Yes. I've taught you, 'No people, no culture.' Herb wanted a culture where people had fun together. To get that fun culture, he needed to hire fun people. So, he created unique pilot interviews. The pilots, who were often ex-military and serious, were brought into a room. The interviewer asked if any pilots would feel more comfortable changing into brown shorts since those would be the Southwest summer uniform. Many pilots declined. But the ones who put on the shorts were identified as matching Kelleher's vision of a fun-loving culture."

"Whoa," said Sam. "Now that's an interview."

"Yes," agreed Brian, "that interview helped build their culture and success. So, can fun affect a company? My answer's yes. And your Ventilator is like Southwest's brown shorts."

"Understood. Should I get another fridge and double the ventilation?"

"Only if you want to violate the 'fun ratio,'" answered Brian.

"Fun ratio?"

"Yes," smiled Brian. "Once you understand company culture should be fun, you must properly ration two types of fun. If you get that ratio wrong, instead of strengthening your culture, you could destroy it."

"Two types of fun?" asked Sam.

"Yes, Sam. And those types don't only determine the success of your company – they can determine the success of your life."

"You've got my attention."

"Good," smiled Brian. "When I was coaching, I found differences how players spent their time having fun. Those differences affected performance. When I started coaching CEOs, I noticed the same trend. That led to the development my '*A/E Success Ratio*.'"

"What do 'A' and 'E' stand for?"

"Each letter," replied Brian, "represents a way a person can spend time having fun. The 'A' stands for 'Achievement' and the 'E' stands for 'Entertainment.'"

Sam gave in to his urge and opened his golden notebook.

"Once I understood the ratio," Brian continued, "I had people log how they spent their time. That's when I discovered more successful people used a higher ratio of Achievement to Entertainment. They spent more time on fun activities that lead to personal or professional achievement, than on fun activities that only produced entertainment."

"Do you have examples of activities?"

"Sure," replied Brian. "For example, athletes who spent more time practicing or training than they did on video games or social media had a higher A/E ratio and always improved. But players who lowered their ratio by spending less time on activities like studying or reading and more on television or texting had less success."

"That makes sense," said Sam. "So, if I understand the ratio, the Ventilator's okay, but there should be more time spent on fun activities that improve people or the company."

"Precisely. Imagine if your staff spent all their time on ideas for the Ventilator at the expense of their work. Sure, it'd be fun, but work wouldn't get done. But you shouldn't get rid of entertainment entirely. People need outlets to blow off some steam, and that's why a culture needs both."

"Like a vent?" smiled Sam.

"Touché," nodded Brian. "The sad part is most people spend little time on achievement. Everyone was born to do something great, but few get the ratio right. Perhaps because entertainment seems easier than achievement, or their sense of drive's been extinguished. But whatever the cause, no one becomes successful binge-watching shows or surfing the lives of other people."

"It's easy to fall into that trap. I've been there, and it's addictive."

"Yes," agreed Brian, "but so's achievement. Reading, training, and programming can be addictive too. That's why the leader should inspire everyone to get the ratio right."

"Am I on the right track?"

"Yes," replied Brian. "Sure you're having fun 'ventilating,' but your projects and hack-a-thons are creative ways to have fun with achievement. I'm not advocating 'all work and no play.' People need entertainment too. So things like your bowling and softball leagues are great and they still promote culture."

"Point taken. I like that ratio idea," said Sam, writing notes.

"Don't just like it. As the crusader, defend it! Create an environment that's fun, but channel that fun into achievement-based activities. When you get the ratio right, Stamina will become a great company."

"That's what I call entertainment," said Sam.

"Let's call it achievement instead."

24

Two Gifts

Before heading to Marcus's office, Brian walked the campus, enjoying the September weather. The silence didn't surprise him. He knew how things worked on a Sunday after a loss.

Brian knew the anticipation a coach felt when searching for a win – and the letdown when he didn't find one. Brian found Marcus sitting at his desk.

"Hey buddy," said Brian.

"Hey, Coach," responded Marcus, "we were soooo close."

"That's how this game works," replied Brian. "One play can make the difference."

"Yeah," said Marcus. "Watching the tape doesn't make it easier."

"It's not supposed to be easier, kid. You're supposed to get better. It's painful to lose. I've had plenty of losses. And that's why I'm here – to continue your coaching 'education.'"

"I wanted to win that first one," said Marcus.

"But not the second one? C'mon. A coach wants to win them all. It's learning to deal with it when you don't."

"Yeah," sighed Marcus. "I know. I checked out the media's take. I'm already on the chopping block."

"Well," said Brian, "there's your first mistake. Don't listen to critics. I saw the game, and not only did you almost beat a Top-25 team, but when you finish grading, you'll find few coaching errors. You're not the first college coach to start out with adversity."

"Is this supposed to make me feel better?"

"I'm not trying to make you feel better," replied Brian. "I want you to feel the pain. The sting of a loss can propel you and the team forward. Just know you aren't the first guy to overcome losing. Heard of John McKay?"

"The USC coach?"

"Yup," said Brian. "When he took over that program, they were ranked sixth in the country."

"His teams were always powerhouses." replied Marcus.

"Not always," said Brian. "That first team went 4–6 and unranked. It took a few more years before his four national championships."

"I didn't know that."

"Yeah," said Brian. "People forget that stuff. How about Florida State legend Bobby Bowden? He didn't just lose his first game as head coach, he lost his first three! Imagine if he gave up because of critics. He wouldn't have his two national championship rings either."

"I'm sorry, Coach," said Marcus. "I know losing's part of the game."

"It is. But how you choose to respond to a loss is the part of your game I want you to improve. Yes, that game was close. But you can't control the way the ball bounces. That's why they call it the 'breaks.' There'll be games when the ball bounces your way too. How will you act then?"

Marcus answered, "I'd be fired up."

"Be careful. That's why I brought you two gifts."

"Two gifts?" repeated Marcus.

"Deuce," replied Brian. "I knew a fighter from the famous Gracie family. He helped me with the hand fighting stuff I taught you. He said he felt pressure to win because of his name. But his father did something interesting. When the fighter won a tournament, his father gave him one gift. But when he lost, he gave him two."

"Why'd he do that?"

"The two gifts symbolized that while victory is good, losing can be more valuable," answered Brian. "The fighter learned to find value in every loss, and told me those losses made him a champion."

Brian pulled out an object connected to a long chain and said, "Here's gift number one."

"What's this?"

"That's something the basketball coach gave me when I got the head coaching job," answered Brian.

"But what *is* it?" asked Marcus, examining the white object.

"That's an antique pull-handle. It's used to flush toilets. This one's from England and made of porcelain."

"And what's it for?" asked Marcus.

"I told you, for flushing toilets."

"No!" chuckled Marcus. "I mean why give it to me?"

"Ohh," joked Brian, "read it and I'll explain."

Marcus saw the word "Next" painted horizontally.

"Next?"

"That's the idea the coach gave me," Brian explained. "He used it to win a bunch of championships too. His motto was 'What's next.' He taught his players after a bad play or even a loss to stay composed, learn from it, and move on to what's next."

"Cool idea," said Marcus. "But what's that got to do with toilets?"

"He told me as his team embraced 'what's next,' some of the players started making a flushing motion after bad plays. They said the action represented 'next' by flushing away the play."

"Ahh," smiled Marcus. "Flush the bad stuff and move on, huh?"

"Yes. But the coach took it further. He didn't only use 'what's next' to move on from bad things – he used it to move on from good things too!"

"From good things?" asked Marcus.

"Yup," replied Brian. "You know, like over-celebration or living on past successes. Those are paralyzing too."

"I like it!"

"Then adopt it," replied Brian. "This handle's for you. It should sit on your desk by your compass and your brick. They're all *cultural reminders*. The handle reminds you not to get too high or too low and look to 'what's next.'"

"I'll do my best. That's why I'm here so early. Since we have a team workout later, I wanted to grade this game before I spend tonight watching film for next week."

"I was worried you'd say that," said Brian as he handed Marcus a 4-by-4-inch black case and said, "That's why I brought gift number two."

Marcus opened the case. Inside was a metal stopwatch encased in black foam. As he examined the timepiece, he recognized a word and said, "Rolex?"

"Uh-huh."

"I can't accept this, Coach" said Marcus. "It's worth a fortune."

"It's worth what a person thinks it's worth," said Brian. "And it's worth giving to my best student. It's a 'Compteur" stopwatch from the 1930s."

"I can't take this."

"You have to," replied Brian. "The worst thing to do is say 'no thanks' when someone gives you a gift. That's true for stopwatches and compliments too. This watch, just like the pull-handle, was given to me. Now I'm passing it down to you from *coach to coach*. That's how the world works. Knowledge and tradition are passed down from coach to coach. And I'm not giving this stuff to you. I'm loaning it to you until you pass it on someday."

"Thanks so much, Coach. You know I like watches."

"I didn't give you the watch to admire it." said Brian. "Use to count your time *and* make your time count. Compteur means 'counter' in French."

Brian took out the watch and clicked it.

"Just like the pull-handle's to remind you to focus on what's next, this stopwatch should remind you to clock out and make time for your family. The biggest mistake of my coaching career wasn't working too little – it was making too little time for Kelly and the girls. This is your reminder not to make the same mistake."

Brian clicked to stop the timer.

"Remember, Marcus, wins and losses will come and go, but you can't have time back with family. Let this watch remind you to carve out time . . . and *make it count.*"

Marcus and Brian sat quietly.

"Thanks for these," started Marcus. "After all my work, I'm questioning myself. I don't want the team to lose hope. I want them to experience winning. Am I doing the right thing?"

"I have an old rule," answered Brian. "If everyone I trust tells me something, even if I don't want to hear it, it's true."

"And?"

"And . . . I'm telling you keep doing what you're doing!" replied Brian. "You can't let one loss undermine everything you've done here. Is anyone else telling you to change?"

"No . . ."

"Then stay the course! Don't listen to the media," said Brian. "Listen to people you trust, and keep going. A great example is John Wooden."

"Wooden?" replied Marcus.

"Yes. You know he built a winning culture that won ten national titles in 12 years, right?"

"Roger that," answered Marcus. "He started every season teaching his players how to put on their socks and shoes, and his practices were planned to the minute."

"Good memory," smiled Brian. "But you're forgetting something."

"What's that?"

"Coach Wooden took 16 years to win his first championship!" Brian exclaimed. "Imagine if he questioned everything after his first season? He didn't change his philosophy. He believed what he was doing and delivered what a successful culture needs – *consistency!*"

Brian continued, "You're building something great here. Yesterday's game proved the team's better than last year. Build a culture that lasts longer than a game or season. Just like Wooden did, build a culture to stand for decades."

Marcus picked up the handle and said, "What's next?"

"That's the spirit," smiled Brian. "Remember, failures will happen. Those failures are neither final nor fatal. The secret isn't if failures happen – it's how you respond to them."

"Thanks, Coach," said Marcus. "You know me. I'm not good at losing."

"That's why you got two gifts."

25

The Rubber Match

"Okay, men!" yelled Marcus. "Everyone gather 'round."

The team assembled in the center of the locker room.

"Before we hear from someone, I want to introduce two people who've had a lot to do with this team's success. You learned a lot of things about each other this season. Some of them," smiled Marcus, "probably should've been kept a secret."

The players laughed.

"But whether things were funny or serious, this team got to know each other. And not just where everyone is from or each other's favorite songs or movies. We went deeper – to future hopes and dreams. I've heard true knowledge is self-knowledge. Well, this team knows itself, and these two men are the ones to thank for it," said Marcus pointing over to Sam and Raj. "Give it up for Sam Raucci and Raj Surendran for creating our Cor Unum app!"

The players applauded.

"Throughout the year, I've tried to motivate you. If you've enjoyed it, thank our guest speaker. This man needs no introduction. He's brought pride to the people of this university, but more importantly, he's positively changed the lives of his players. I know because I'm one of them. Coach Knight didn't just change my life – he saved it!"

Marcus continued, "This is our last home game. Instead of hearing from me, you'll listen to the master. Everyone give your attention to Coach Knight!"

Dressed in home uniforms with a Cor Unum patch on the left chest, the players faced Brian.

"Alright men," said Brian, "it's been a long time since I addressed a team in this locker room. I've coached in this stadium against Top 10 teams and when championships were on the line. There've been a lot of big games, but I believe this is the biggest game I'll ever be part of!"

"Maybe because you are 5–4 right now, you don't think it's a big game. You're dead wrong!" yelled Brian.

"When you signed with this school, you became part of the greatest tradition in sports. And that's a tradition of winning . . . a tradition I hold in the utmost regard. And today's your chance to *uphold that tradition*. A win today guarantees a winning season and a bowl invite. A win today can prove everyone who counted us out wrong. But most importantly, a win today lets you honor those who've created our winning tradition."

"Because this is my most important pregame speech," Brian continued, "I'll share a story about the most important choice you'll ever make. I don't know if you know the history here, but this school wasn't always a national powerhouse. In fact, back in the 1920s and '30s, this school couldn't book a game. No one wanted to play us because no one ever heard of us!"

Brian lowered his volume.

"Just a few games changed this school forever. Because today can be one of those games, I'll tell you about the one that got it all started."

Brian paused and began. "Imagine spending four years never getting into a game. You never played a down and with only one game left, instead of the call to play, you get the worst call imaginable. That's what happened during Patrick Grayson's final week of football. Pat was called to the coach's office and notified that his father had died. Since Pat would head home and miss his final game, the coach asked if there was *anything* he could do. Pat answered, 'Coach, it'd be great during your pregame talk to tell the team to win for my dad.' The coach agreed, and

Pat left for the funeral. The week of practice went as usual. On game day, the coach was nervous for two reasons – he wanted to give a good talk to honor Pat's dad, and his tiny school was playing the best team in the country."

"The team assembled in this very locker room. The coach was in the office right there," Brian said, pointing, "preparing his speech when the unthinkable happened. Pat Grayson walked into that office and closed the door! 'Pat!' the coach said, 'What're you doing here? Shouldn't you be home?' Pat said, 'No, coach, after talking to my mother, she believed I should be here today.' The coach was surprised by something else. Pat was dressed to play! The coach said, 'Pat, it's great you're here, but why're you dressed?' Pat said, 'Coach, remember when you asked if you could do '*anything*'?' The coach said, 'Yes, your father's speech is ready.' Then Pat said, 'No, Coach, I'm not asking about a speech. I'm asking for a chance to play.' The coach was stunned. 'Play?' he said, 'Pat, you've never played a down, and this is the biggest game in school history.' Pat slumped and the coach reconsidered and said, 'But . . . you've worked hard for four years, so you've earned it. Late in the game I'll get you in on a kickoff.' Pat confidently replied, 'Coach, I don't want to get in the game, I want the ball.' Because of Pat's situation, the coach relented and said, 'Okay . . . one play.'"

"Game day was colder than it is today," said Brian as he pointed toward the field. "And locked in a 0–0 battle, our tiny team was holding its own, when tragedy struck. The star halfback fractured his leg. Scrambling for a replacement, the coach yelled, 'Grayson get in there!' On the next play, Pat Grayson shocked everyone and ran for 6 yards. The promise honored, Pat began to jog off the field, but the coach yelled, 'Stay on, stay on!'"

"The rest is the stuff of legend," smiled Brian. "Pat Grayson played the game of his life. He finished with over 100 yards rushing and scored the only touchdown to lead this school to the 7–0 victory that put us on the map forever."

"After the game it was pandemonium in here," said Brian, scanning the room. "Players were celebrating like crazy, but there was one person who wasn't. The coach couldn't take it anymore. He pulled Pat into his office and asked, 'Pat! What was that? You've been here four years! How do you explain your performance?' Pat said, 'Coach, today's performance was for my dad.' The coach replied, 'That doesn't explain anything.' Then Pat asked, 'Did you ever meet my dad?' The coach answered, 'No I never did.'"

"'You never met him, because years ago, my dad was injured and lost his sight. Because he could no longer see, he never came to a game. But my mother told me, 'Patty, get in that game and give your all because this isn't just your last game, it's the last game your daddy gets to see you play.'"

You could hear a pin drop.

"Whether you've heard that story or not," Brian shouted, "it's not about the story, it's about the *choice*. Just like Pat Grayson had, you make the same choice today. And that choice won't just decide this game, it'll decide what happens the rest of your life! And what's that choice? It's simple – are you going to *hold back*, or are you going to *go all out*? If anything's holding you back, today's the day to let it go – the day to go . . . *all* . . . *out*! Your family and fans are watching. Go out there and protect our tradition!"

Brian finished and then Marcus yelled, "Alright men . . . helmets on!"

As the players began snapping their helmets into place, Sam saw many of them were covered in the stickers he designed.

The team assembled behind Marcus at the edge of the tunnel where they would rush onto the field. The players were a tightly packed wall of equipment, muscle, and adrenalin, each one hitting his right fist on the Cor Unum patch in a two-beat count.

Marcus addressed his team.

"Alright! For some of you, this is your last game in here. Forget that and remember back to before you got here. Remember the day you signed to come to this school? Remember that player? Remember how excited you were to wear this uniform? Well, I need that player here today. I need him right now!"

The players helmets were nodding in unison.

"Put your fingers on your neck! You feel that? *You . . . feel . . . that?* That's Cor Unum, baby! One heart! The world's waiting for us out there. Let's go get 'em!"

Marcus and the team sprinted onto the field.

As the team ran onto the field, Brian, Sam, and Raj heard the crowd erupt. They stood savoring the powerful sports moment.

Sam said to Brian, "Amazing story, Coach. Great job."

"Thanks," replied Brian. "I went all out."

"That was one of the coolest things ever!" said Raj, giving Brian a high ten. "I know a lot of football history here. That story about Pat Grayson . . . I've heard different versions. Was that true?"

Brian smiled and said, "Does it matter?"

"What do you mean?" asked Raj.

"Right in this spot," replied Brian, "an old coach once told me it doesn't matter if a story's true – *it only matters if it works.*"

Raj turned to Sam and said, "I hope it works for us."

26

The Holiday Party

The Stamina staff and their families were enjoying the holiday party.

After go-kart racing, everyone moved into the private party room. As they compared ugly Christmas sweaters, the noise of the group mixed with the holiday music of DJ Ben. While people grabbed food from the buffet, Sam moved from table to table greeting everyone. Sam appeared confident and happy, but as the clock ticked closer to 7:30 p.m., the knot in his stomach tightened.

Melissa kept the event on schedule. She and Dana had worked hard organizing the event. Around 7 p.m., Melissa let Sam know Brian had arrived, but before Sam could greet him, he got stuck at the photo booth area. For the next 25 minutes, Sam changed into funny outfits and took photos with the team. Sam glanced over and saw Brian talking to his mother at the back of the room. Sam was glad Brian had met his mom, and hoped to introduce them properly.

At the photo booth, Sam lost track of time. At 7:30, Melissa told Sam to stay on schedule. "Good thing the lawyer's running this thing," Sam thought and made his way to the front of the room. Melissa handed him the microphone and whispered, "Good luck." Sam asked everyone to take their seats. After a minute, Sam began the speech he'd practiced for weeks.

"Good evening," began Sam. "If we haven't met, I'm Sam Raucci, the founder of Stamina, and I want to welcome everyone to the holiday party!"

The group applauded.

"To begin, I have two questions. Number one, is everyone having a good time in those ugly sweaters?"

The people cheered again.

"And number two, is anybody else nervous to get on the road with some of these people after what you saw tonight?"

The crowd broke into laughter.

"I want to thank everyone for being here tonight," Sam continued. "And I mean *everyone*, because each of you has played a part in the great news. With almost a month still left in the year, Stamina has already had its best year ever!"

Everyone cheered.

"Stamina has had such a turnaround, whether you work onsite or remotely, you can't help but notice. And our customers have noticed too. In fact, I've been asked by so many how we got so much better, I kept repeating the same story. Since I've told it so often, I'm telling it again tonight."

Sam paused.

"In 1955, a 10-foot-tall concrete statue of Buddha was being moved to a new location in Thailand. The statue was moving because its ruined temple had become littered with garbage, and the statue attracted no attention. When the movers tried to lift it from the podium, the statue tipped and fell! One of the workers noticed something shining where some concrete had chipped away. When the movers chipped off more concrete, they realized the statue was made of gold! They discovered what's called the 'Golden Buddha.'"

"Work was halted," Sam continued, "and the authorities investigated. Here's what they found: In the late 1700s, this golden statue was covered in concrete to hide it from Burmese invaders who were attacking the city. Because most people were driven from the area, the truth inside the statue was forgotten – for over 200 years."

"Today," Sam continued, "the Golden Buddha is displayed in a beautiful temple in Bangkok so all 5.5 tons of the 18K gold can be appreciated. In case you're wondering, since an ounce of gold costs $1,800, the statue's street value is almost a half a billion dollars!"

A few of the crowd gasped.

"So, why do I tell our customers that story? Because Stamina's just like that statue – we had gold inside, but forgot it was there. And I take full responsibility for that. I was the one who put the concrete over the real gold of Stamina – our people. But we've spent the last year chipping away and letting our people shine. Next year, the world will see our greatness and you'll never be forgotten again."

Sam paused for cheers.

"That story's powerful because the gold underneath was always there – *we just didn't recognize it*. Because I won't make the same mistake, I'm going to recognize some gold now."

Melissa handed a glass award to Sam.

"Every organization needs a code – a set of principles," began Sam. "And when someone lives according to those values, they should be celebrated. Tonight, I'm introducing the Stamina Core Value Awards by celebrating four people who've lived our core values at the highest level."

Sam looked at the award.

"Can Brandon Gallas stand up, please? The first core value at Stamina is 'Work Hard.' And at Stamina, we don't measure this core value in the number of hours you work or the effort you put into our projects. We look deeper – into your potential. Some people discover they *can* work hard, but this year Brandon found out *how hard* he can work. As the new head of the sales team, Brandon accepted a leadership role and was directly responsible for our highest earnings ever. Brandon has worked hard – and that's why I'm proud to announce the Work Hard Core Value Award goes to Brandon Gallas!" Sam said as he motioned Brandon up front to accept his award. After Sam gave Brandon a patented Stamina high ten and walked back to his seat, Melissa handed Sam another award.

"Can Shelly Tremble please stand?" requested Sam as applause restarted. "If you know Shelly, it's no surprise she won our 'Play Hard' award. That doesn't mean Shelly's just *having* fun – Shelly *makes work fun* for everyone. Shelly brought her infectious energy to our bowling and softball teams and developed the Stamina high ten, which I hope you're using at home too. And playing hard doesn't mean Shelly doesn't work – she's received positive feedback from our customers too. So, give it up for the Play Hard Core Value Award winner, Shelly Tremble!" Shelly danced up to collect her award as she pumped up the crowd. She gave Sam a high ten and when she sat, Sam was ready with the next award.

"Can Lealon Gamble please stand up? If you don't know, Lealon is affectionately known as 'The Intern,'" Sam grinned as Lealon nodded his head, laughing. "The next award is for 'Being Curious.' You've probably heard 'curiosity killed the cat,' as if curiosity's a bad idea. I've heard your life's a reflection of your questions. At Stamina, we don't discourage questions – *we mandate them.* This year, at our first hack-a-thon, Lealon asked a question that led to new products and revenue for the company! Since he's now full-time, he's kept up that curiosity, and has continued to push Stamina forward. My hope is that winning this award doesn't stop his questions, but leads to more. Let's hear it for the Be Curious Core Value Award winner, Lealon Gamble!" Lealon rushed up and collected his high ten award, and Melissa handed Sam another trophy.

"Can I have Ivette Bonnes stand, please?"

Ivette stood to more applause.

"Your parents probably told you," began Sam, "to be nice. I'm sure they said this when nice was the last thing you felt like being."

The crowd laughed.

"Stamina's fourth core value is 'Be Nice,' and that's also the last thing anyone feels like doing with a disgruntled customer or disagreeing teammate. Being nice isn't easy, but being nice is the right thing to do. Ivette has been a trooper for us in customer service. Her peaceful and easygoing personality not only calms the occasional angry customer, but our new service mantra won her this award. Months ago, Dana ran into my office saying, 'You know what Ivette just said?'" Sam said, getting some laughs with his impersonation of Dana. "'At Stamina, we don't sell memberships, *we build relationships*.' That changed the game for us, so big cheers for the Be Nice Core Value Award winner, Ivette Bonnes!" Because Ivette was crying, she skipped the high ten and gave Sam a hug. As she held her award up for the crowd, Melissa handed Sam a plaque.

"There's one final award," said Sam. "Stamina was created to breathe life into companies – to charge them up, and keep them charged for the future. Well, there are people who do that for our company too. Over the last three quarters, we've given out a Hard Charger Award to the person who's charged up the people around them. The recipient of this final award has done that and more.

He's led the way bringing all of us together, and gives positive support to anyone who needs it. This man spent long hours designing new programs while *making everyone here better*. I'm thankful he works for Stamina, but even more thankful he's my friend. The Hard Charger of the Year Award goes to our mad scientist . . . our house comedian . . . Raj Surendran!"

Everyone gave Raj a standing ovation.

"To finish," began Sam, "I have two quick requests. First, there's one person I must single out or I wouldn't forgive myself. Honey, can you please come up here?" As Melissa walked around the table, the crowd's cheers thoroughly embarrassed her, just as Sam planned.

"You might know that this is my wife, Melissa. But you might not know that Melissa wasn't involved with our company – and that upset me. Although we hit our highest numbers, I'm happier now because Melissa joined our team."

Sam's voice cracked as he looked at her. "Melissa, you've taught me that working with my wife can be fun, and Stamina can serve a bigger purpose."

Sam addressed the group. "Melissa's been trying to figure out her role at Stamina. And today I'm proud to announce her official title . . . introducing our Director of Social Impact, Melissa Raucci!"

The group applauded and Melissa hugged Sam.

"At Stamina we create games to improve communication," Sam said. "Melissa understands that no one likes an unfair game. Her division's committed to fighting for equal opportunity, access, and respect for all workers in our community. Melissa will oversee Stamina's social initiatives, and we're excited to announce she's created a partnership with the Green Valley shelter. Stamina will bring our technology to the homeless in our area. Since the number one way to end homelessness is job creation, we're committed to doing our part." Melissa gave Sam a kiss, and the crowd cheered louder.

"Before you sit," Sam started, "I have one last thing. I want to recognize everyone here, so please come up to the dance floor."

The group assembled on the floor.

"Please form a circle around me," Sam said as they huddled up.

"Ok, now tighten up," Sam said, and the circle contracted.

"Now, put your arms over the person's shoulders next to you."

The group interlinked their arms. Sam stood in the center.

"I started with the Golden Buddha, and how the 'gold' of Stamina is our people. I'll finish by explaining your responsibility to protect that gold."

Sam slowly turned, addressing everyone.

"You may know, the redwood tree is one of the tallest trees in the world. In fact, redwoods grow over 250 feet high and are thousands of years old. But you might not know about the redwood's roots. Because of its size and height, you might think those roots would dive deep in the ground. But they don't – redwood roots only go a dozen feet down! So how can the redwood stand so tall in the challenging California winds, floods, and earthquakes? The secret isn't how deep a redwood grows – it's how closely redwoods grow *together*. Redwoods don't need deep roots, because just like your arms right now, the redwoods intertwine and support each other. The redwoods stand so tall because they've learned to *stand together*."

"Look around you," finished Sam. "Just like the redwood, Stamina's going to stand tall because we have a great team of people supporting each other. The way Stamina will climb higher next year will be continuing to *lift each other up.*"

27

The Letter

"How do you think this'll go, Coach?" said Marcus, looking at the front door.

"It'll be up to him, kid," replied Brian.

"There he is," said Marcus, as Sam walked into Trackside. "I guess we'll find out."

Sam saw Brian's classic double-arm wave. As Sam approached, he wondered why Marcus and Brian were seated on one side of the table, but dismissed the notion and sat across from them.

"Hey guys!" said Sam.

Brian and Marcus just smiled and didn't respond.

"Before I forget," said Sam, "Congrats on the bowl bid, Coach."

Marcus replied, "Thanks Sam. We're all so happy. Couldn't have done it without your help."

"I couldn't have gotten another meeting with the university without your help either. We pitched them last week and nailed it. I'm confident we're getting a shot."

"That's great," replied Marcus.

Sam gave a box to Brian and said, "Hello to you too, Coach. Here's your present from the party. You left early and I wanted you to have it."

"Thanks Sam. Should I open it?"

"Sure," said Sam.

Brian unwrapped it and found a Stamina basketball jersey inside. "Wow," said Brian. "This is first-class."

"It's for the upcoming basketball league. Check out the back."

There were five embroidered letters spelling "Coach."

"The team voted you coach. Hope you don't mind," said Sam.

"Not at all, Sam." Brian smiled as he looked over at Marcus.

Marcus nodded at Brian and said, "This is as good time as any."

Both men looked back at Sam, but neither spoke.

"Okay, what's up, guys?" asked Sam. "Now you two look like you're up to something."

"Sam," began Brian, "since your holiday party last week, I've wondered how to approach this – so I'm just gonna go for it. . . . Why didn't you ever tell me who your birth father was?"

Sam crinkled his brow and stammered, "I . . . uhh . . . I never thought it was important."

Brian and Marcus just looked back at Sam. Sam realized they were both in on this.

Sam continued, "My real dad died before I was born. I never knew him."

Brian said, "I know, and I'm sorry. We don't want to catch you off guard and I don't want this stirring things the wrong way."

Sam looked away and crossed his arms.

"But didn't you ever think I might've known him?" asked Brian.

"It crossed my mind, but when I saw the team photos at your house, they weren't the years my father played here. So I didn't bring it up."

"Ahh," said Brian looking at Marcus. "Those photos were my head coaching years. But I coached here before that."

Sam was uncomfortable where this was going. He blurted out, "I never even found out who he was until I was 10 and playing sports. People started comparing me to him, so my mom told me the truth. It hasn't been a positive subject."

Sam took a deep breath.

"And if I ever brought him up, my mom would get so upset, it filled me with resentment. And it wasn't fair to my dad who raised me. He's been there my whole life, and helped me out so much . . . I let it go."

Marcus and Brian sat listening.

"Where's this coming from anyway? I saw you talking to my mom at the party. Did she put you up to this?"

"Yes, I talked to her," answered Brian, "But no, she didn't put me up to anything. Bringing it up was my idea, because we were both unsure whether to give you what I have for you. But we decided I should."

"Give me what?" Sam said agitated.

Brian pulled out a letter.

"Before we go any further, kid, this will explain," said Brian as he handed Sam the envelope.

Because it was addressed to Brian, Sam didn't know what to do.

"Open it," said Brian.

Sam opened the envelope, and removed the paper inside. Sam unfolded it and read the handwritten print:

Coach,

Since I'm graduating this year, my father told me it's important to thank the people who've helped me. Because you're one of my biggest influences, I wanted to thank you.

I cannot believe my five years at the university are almost over. The thing I'll miss most is playing with the "Three Musketeers," but your stories are a close second. This season was an amazing finish and reminded me of the beginning. From the time you came to our house to recruit me, I knew this was the place for me and you were the coach who'd help me reach my dreams.

Now that I've been drafted to the NFL, thanks for keeping that promise. You never gave up on me, and even through injury and personal challenges, you never let me quit. I'll never forget it.

The thing I thank you for most isn't football. You made me a better player, but you also made me a better person. I'll use your lessons in the NFL, but now I'll need them off the field more than ever. We haven't told anyone yet, but Christine's pregnant! We couldn't be more excited. Whether it's a boy or girl, I know this kid will be a star. (But to be honest, I hope it's a boy!)

I wanted you to be the first to know, and look forward to your wisdom to help me make sure my child grows up right. When we announce it, I'm planning on asking Marcus to be the godfather too. Although we'll be enemies on Sundays, he'll always be the friend I trust most.

Thanks for everything, Coach. I'll do my best to make you proud.

Your biggest fan,

Charlie Powell

Sam processed what his birth father had written.

"If you look at the date," began Brian, "it's post-marked the day before his accident."

Sam carefully placed the letter in the envelope. Sam's lips were pursing and he saw tears in Marcus's eyes.

Feeling the emotion, Brian said, "Sam, we didn't want to upset you. Your mother and I think you know who your dad was, but not how he lived. I can't think of two better people to tell you about him than us."

"All of this . . ." Sam said, "us working together at Stamina . . . this wasn't a setup between you and my mom, was it?"

"No, Sam," said Brian and Marcus simultaneously.

"We're as shocked as you are," said Marcus.

"I can't explain what pulled the three of us together," began Brian. "I don't know if it's the universe righting itself or not, but we're here now. We were brought together for a reason – a deeper meaning behind why we met. I've been thinking so much since the party, it's driving me crazy."

"What do you think?" asked Sam.

"At first, I thought we connected to close some loop. Maybe even Charlie was up there pushing us together."

Sam and Marcus listened.

"But now I think we met to help each other. And I believe this happened because I needed help."

Marcus said, "C'mon, Coach, I brought you in to help me. When I got the job, I was lost."

"You?" interrupted Sam, "I had the company that was falling part. I needed the help."

"No," replied Brian. "As challenged as you both were, there were things I was covering up. Things I wasn't honest about with either of you."

"What do you mean?" asked Marcus.

"I wasn't in a good place mentally. I was drinking too much, and wasn't taking care of myself. But my problem wasn't the drinking or eating – those were symptoms of the problem. I was self-medicating for loneliness. I didn't feel I mattered anymore."

"That's not true," said Marcus.

"No way," chimed Sam.

Brian nodded. "Don't get nuts here, guys. I feel better now, and that's why I think we've found each other. I've shared a lot of stories, but there's one I've never told anyone. Not because I didn't want to, but because I wasn't sure what it meant . . . until now."

Brian began.

"A prince lived in a castle. Because he was rich and could own anything, he lacked drive. The prince learned of a guru who had what no one possessed: the answer to any question. The prince set out atop his finest horse to find this guru. The journey was harsh – the prince and horse crossed rivers, climbed mountains, and braved deserts searching for this mythical guru. After two years, the prince found the guru seated in a temple on the highest mountain. The prince approached and asked, 'What's the one thing that cannot be bought, but can provide a lifetime of fulfillment?' After hours in thought, the guru had his answer. The guru walked over to the prince's horse. Although it was tired and sore, it still stood steadfast and waiting. The wise man said to the prince, 'You didn't need to come so far to ask your question. The answer's been under you your entire journey. *You just had to ask your horse.*'"

Brian looked at Marcus and Sam.

"Good one, right? I've thought about it for years, never sure of the moral. I used to think maybe it was unconditional service without complaint? Or having a job that served a noble purpose?"

Brian paused.

"There was another time in my life when I hit rock bottom. Like this time, someone was brought into my life in a way I can't explain. Seeing your mom last week reminded me of that person and the horse story again. And I was reminded of the solution I found during that difficult time."

Brian looked upward and continued, "I think the horse represents being a coach – taking someone where they want to go without worrying about yourself – selflessly carrying someone forward no matter what it takes. I think we connected to remind me I'm still that horse and this old horse still has value."

Brian inhaled.

"I'd given up when Kelly died. I felt so alone. But you two have given me purpose again – a chance to use what I've learned and feel I still have something to contribute. So you may have thought I've had answers for you, but you both had the answer for me. *Because everyone always needs a coach, a coach is always needed.*"

Tears welled in his eyes as he said, "So thank you for being someone for this old coach to help."

Marcus puts his hand on Brian's and said, "You'll never be alone, Coach."

Sam put his hand on top of Marcus's and said, "*We are family.*"

The race of life can do interesting things to people.

All three men drove home alone that night. One was excited because he knew what was next. Another was optimistic because he had a lot of clues. But the one who stopped off for a six-pack of seltzer realized he was energized because a coach's help is always needed.

One race in the middle. One race starting. One race almost run.

One heart.

Acknowledgments

Now that you've finished *High Ten*, you should know people are the most important part of your culture. Just like you cannot have a culture without people, an author learns the same is true for an acknowledgments page.

No people, no culture.

No people, no acknowledgments.

An important exercise in this book was when the staff at Stamina did an inventory of all the people who made up their culture. For an author, writing an acknowledgments page is the same exercise and just as difficult.

Writing the acknowledgments is energizing because it forces you to recognize the cultures of which you have been part. But this process also creates anxiety because just like the people in the story, you don't want to leave anyone out.

Who you are and the culture you are part of is a reflection of your "gang." If all the names listed here are a reflection of me, then I am a happy person.

Now I am going to give them some High Tens.

Sam Caucci: The CEO of 1Huddle, who is the inspiration behind the main character in the story. It has been a pleasure to work alongside Sam and be pushed by him because he is a real "Hard Charger."

Scott Altizer: The college athletic director who made sure all of my timelines and coach job descriptions and challenges were accurate. Since he was also my college roommate, he had some great insights about our old culture too.

Dr. Rob Gilbert: The professor and speaker whom I am proud to call my mentor. Of his thousands of lessons, perhaps the biggest was that everyone loves a story. That led to my hunt for stories and ways to share them for the last 20 years.

Martin Rooney Sr.: My dad, who has read just about every paper I have written since I was 10 years old. Thank goodness I can always rely on his grammar education and candor he got from my grandparents.

Bill Parisi: The entrepreneur who changed my lenses so I could see the values, mission, and vision necessary to build a business, team, and culture.

Chris Olsen: The football coach who offered me the opportunity to put my culture ideas to the test. The decade of Wayne Hills teams led to many of my greatest sport moments.

Nick Barringer: The Army Ranger, PhD, and RD and now West Point professor who gave me an all-access view into the culture of the elite soldiers few have seen.

Jim Miller: The UFC fighter with the most fights in UFC history who proved to me you don't have to have a big team to still have a great culture.

Todd Hays: The Olympic medalist and coach and great friend who taught me what it means to be a teammate and how not only to create big visions, but how to make them a reality.

The following names are the people who have helped me over the last 30 years to understand culture. They have helped form my vision, battled alongside me on my mission, and been part of some amazing rituals and moments that resulted on the quest for a great culture. They have helped me "level up" by forcing me to "raise the lid" on my expectations for myself:

Bill Scarola, Chris Poirier (and all the great people at Perform Better), Tony Caterisano, Renzo Gracie, Teimoc Johnston-Ono, Jeffrey Gitomer, Erik Piispa, Darren Biehler, Russ Campbell, Bill Pierce, Kristopher Wazaney, Vince Corrado, Steve Leo, Mark Williams, Brandon Wood, John Cirilo, Joe Kenn, Sal Alosi, Dan Quinn, Jerry Palmieri, Jason Garrett, Tom Myslinski, Dave Tate, Joe DeFranco, Chip Morton, Mark Uyeyama, Scott Goodale, James Jankiewicz, Harrison Bernstein, Larry Bock, Jim Naugle, Dan Payne, Brian Mackler, Alan Herman, Dave Butz, Jason Chayut, Rich Sadiv, Dan Henderson, Steve Krebs, Brian Saxton, Christian Jund, Todd Durkin, Alwyn Cosgrove, Mike Boyle, Adam Bornstein, John Berardi, Lee Burton, Gunnar Peterson, Mark Verstegen, Marc Lebert, Peter Twist, Ingrid Marcum, Chad Landers, Scott Caulfield, Chris Adams, Gunnar Petersen, Jesse Chapman, Corey Smallwood, Shawn Powell, Steve Datte, Mike Clark, Corey Beasley, Tarek Chouja, Thomas Plummer, Bobby Cappuccio, Kevin Wright, Adam Rice, Bedros Keuilian, Craig Ballantyne, Nate Green, Gail Cassidy, Scott Paltos, Abdallah Alawadi, Neal Wolfson, Jeff Bregman, Alicia Saldivar, Neal Pire, Braulio Estima, Lee Miller, Mark Serao, Chris Vaglio, John Gallino, Ginger Leach, Billy Felice, Shauna Rohbock, Valerie Fleming, Greg Olsen, Kevin Olsen, Chris Long, Bobby Smith, Luke Petitgout, Rich Seubert, Gheorghe Muresan, Kirsten Kincade, Brian Toal, Justin Trattou, Dan Miller, Frankie Edgar, Ricardo Almeida, Chris Simms, Matt Simms, Molly Creamer, Rolles Gracie, Roger Gracie, Kyra Gracie, Igor Gracie, Luca Atalla, Alan Teo, Dave Maver, Sean Alvarez, Joe Sampieri, Gene Dunn, Adam Singer, Jamal Paterson, Antti Nurmi, Shintaro Higashi, Arthur Canario, Jimmy Vennitti, Barry Friedberg, Celita

Schutz, Gianni Grippo, Lucas Noonan, Charlie Hoffhine, Mike Springer, Ralph Mirabelli, Andrew Tucker, Rich Venditti, John Naphor, Luis Vasquez, John Derent, Ed Tejada, Rich Thurston, Keith Gallas, Brian Roberts, Mike Parillo, Patrick Gray, Kelly Gray, Richie Mendoza, John Praino, Phil Squatrito, Keith Jeffrey, Tom Robertson, Luka Hocevar, John Annillo, Mike Sobczak, Kian Ameli, Michelle Kelly, Michael Soos, Johannes "Hatsolo" Hattunen, Petri Rasanen, Rob Broeckx, Cory Fernandes, Gio Grassi, Josh Jirgal, Zach Even-Esh, Derek and Jaime Rauscher, Linda and Tero Puukko, Jen and Allen Andreoli, Greg and Pam O'Connor, Greg Gonzalez, Jason Hall, and Dennis Rasmussen.

Special thanks to my TFW team and global network. I would never have been able to learn the lessons in this book if not for their faith in me and the Training for Warriors program. And perhaps the cultural aspect for which I am most proud is we call ourselves the "Familia."

My thanks to all the folks at Wiley, especially senior editor Zachary Schisgal, who, based on the success of *Coach to Coach*, gave me a second swing at the plate.

Cultures are passed down from generation to generation. Big thanks to my parents, Marty and Jeanne, for not only pushing me forward, but never letting me forget where I came from. And special thanks to my parents-in-law, Roger and Michelle, who have helped create some special traditions in my life.

Finally, perhaps the biggest lesson from this book is that culture starts in your own home. I am so grateful for Team Rooney, made up of my wife, Amanda, and our four daughters: Sofia, Kristina, Keira, and Sasha. Thanks most of all to the "Roondogs" for putting up with a coach for a husband and father and for being my biggest supporters in my life's work.

About the Author

Martin Rooney is an internationally recognized coach, sought-after presenter, and best-selling author. A former U.S. bobsledder, Division I track athlete, Judo black belt, record-setting powerlifter, and two-time Guinness World Record holder, Martin is now on a mission to create a world of better coaches. As founder of the global fitness organization Training for Warriors and the former COO of the Parisi Speed School, he has helped create two business cultures that have positively affected millions of people worldwide.

Over the last 20 years, Martin has adventured to over 35 countries and coached hundreds of athletes from the NFL, MLB, UFC, NBA, and WNBA; numerous Olympic medalists; All-Americans; and World Champions. In addition to professional athletes, he has coached hundreds of high school teams with athletes who have gone on to compete at numerous top Division I colleges across the United States. He has also spent a decade testing the culture-building principles in this book as a youth, middle school, and high school track coach.

Martin has shared his *High Ten* philosophy with Fortune 500 companies such as Marriott International, Nike, Prudential, and Hasbro; military organizations such as the Army Rangers, Army Airborne, and the Navy Seals; NFL teams such as the New York Jets, Cincinnati Bengals, Carolina Panthers, and New York Giants; and universities such as Arizona State University, University of Alabama, Oregon State University, Rutgers University, Auburn University, Brown University, and West Point.

Martin lives in North Carolina with Team Rooney, composed of his wife, Amanda, and their four daughters, Sofia, Kristina, Keira, and Sasha.

Does Your Team or Business Need a Culture Coach?

Martin delivers high-energy keynotes and game-changing half-day or full-day culture and coaching workshops for companies and associations around the world. For more information or to contact Martin directly, please visit www.coachinggreatness.com or email him at Martin@ CoachingGreatness.com.

About the Company

This book may be a fictional account of a fictitious business, but Stamina is based on a very real company called 1Huddle. Headquartered in Newark, New Jersey, 1Huddle is a workforce tech startup that uses games to inspire and level up workers in every industry. 1Huddle works with leading brands from across the globe to create better, more equitable organizational cultures that are ready to handle any disruption the future of work has in store. Through the use of science-backed, quick-burst mobile games, 1Huddle is transforming the way companies worldwide tackle company culture and worker development.

So if you want to learn more and actually get your hands on 1Huddle's culture-building game platform, then you can start playing the *High Ten* game now by going to http://www.1huddle.co/highten.